ACTION WEALTH GUIDE TO

FINANCIAL LITERACY
FOR TEENS & THEIR PARENTS

HOW TO MAKE, MANAGE, MULTIPLY AND PROTECT YOUR MONEY

GEOFFREY SEMAGANDA

DEDICATION

This book is dedicated to my father who prepared me to become a man from the age of five, and even though we parted so early I was ready to take care of myself from the age of 12 and to become the person I am today. Love you Dad, and thank you (RIP). And to my mother—thank you for always believing in me.

To my Africa family who gave me the licence to go out and discover a new world as well as the freedom to keep trying different business ideas for so many years.

To all my friends who have dared to try something new and who have shown the courage to be different. To the child I once was, and to every adult I see who plays with ideas in a child-like spirit.

To my two beautiful daughters, Jonell Semaganda and Tamiya Semaganda, for inspiring me to write this book: I love you very much.

To Yvonne Puschel: thank you for being there for our girls.

INSTRUCTOR'S GUIDE

For our Financial Literacy for Teens and Their Parents *Instructor's Guide*, please email:

Guide@FinancialLiteracyForTeens.com

Or visit:

www.FinancialLiteracyForTeens.com.

TABLE OF CONTENTS

AUTHOR'S NOTES

Lacking Needed Skills

I am a father of two daughters – ages fourteen and eight. Sometimes I look at them and wonder if we, as their parents, are providing enough tools and instruction for them to compete in our highly competitive society. I conduct workshops and seminars all over the world, as well as personal consulting. My primary concern is that young people today are not equipped with the skills needed to compete on the world stage. They lack the skills and the needed attitudes to succeed in the real world.

If you look at the world today, you will see that youth unemployment has almost doubled in the past decade. I live in the United Kingdom, and Europe has one of the highest youth unemployment figures in the developed world. In other regions, such as Asia and Africa, it's even worse. The major problem is that the educational system is not doing the job in helping young people to develop the attitudes necessary for them to succeed.

Our educational system is not conveying these aspects to children at an early age. As a result, after more than 24,000 hours of education (an average for a student spending twelve years in school) 80% will graduate but they won't have any idea what they're going to do and won't even know how to figure it out. I find this fact extremely disturbing. Our schools are doing little or nothing to prepare kids for their predictable destination, and that is the *world of work*. I'm not saying that all educational systems are useless, but I do believe that they should be upgraded to meet today's demands for a modern world.

In this revolutionary age of modern technology, we are still stuck in the old system of the past.

The Old System

The old system was where parents told their children to study hard, get good grades, and get a good job with a good company that will provide excellent benefits. Then that job would hold them for a lifetime, after which they could retire with a pension. The truth of the matter is that those days are gone forever.

How can we as parents make sure that we are doing the right thing to help our children to be able to compete out there in today's world? After all, the world we live in is much more difficult and complex than the one that this generation of parents grew up in. It's different; it's much more competitive. In today's society you are competing with the whole world, not just with those who are in your own vicinity.

Begin with Money and Finances

I think that the best way to start the subject of equipping our children with the right survival tools for life is to discuss money and finances. When you try to talk to young people about their lives 20 or 30 years from now, they don't pay much attention. Growing older is an abstract concept for them. But when it comes to money, it's actually very clear to them.

When you tell a seven-year-old that if he will perform certain chores, you will pay him a dollar, this child will understand the concept. He will be motivated because of that monetary payment—the reward, so to speak. So this is where we will begin. We are addressing the subject of financial literacy for teenagers and their parents.

This book is designed to provide parents with tips and ideas regarding money and their children. It will provide the foundation to help parents understand the world that their children are facing. This book is also designed to give young people the information and tools needed to understand the world of finance. It will encourage them to take responsibility for their lives.

Begin Financial Education Early

Many young people today are unable to purchase their first home because it's so expensive. They end up living at home under their parents' roof until they are thirty or even older. This had not been the case for those of past generations. It's vital for parents to begin the financial education of their children early on in life.

Our kids must learn that they will be paid based on the value they bring to the marketplace. This discussion must begin at home when the children are young. Once they understand the important concepts about money and finances, they will begin to enjoy school more— because now they will understand why they are getting their education. Everything will begin to make more sense to them.

Additionally, such knowledge will help them to take more responsibility, and to develop a sense of maturity. They will learn how to make money, manage money, multiply money, and protect money.

Those people who we see as a success in today's world; most of them started young. Their parents did a fantastic job of encouraging them to launch out early on. As we view the business world today, there is no denying that parents have a very big role to play in preparing their children. Let's face it—schools cannot fully equip our children for life; the school systems are letting us down.

Let me be quick to add here that I am not saying that money and finances constitute a total answer to what our teens will need in order to enter the workforce. Here is a list of other attributes that all of us parents (those of us who go to work every day) know will be necessary to hold down a job in any society:

- Critical Thinking
- Writing
- Problem Solving
- People Skills
- Communication
- Ability to Access Knowledge
- Computer Technology Skills
- Interviewing Skills
- Public Speaking
- Strong Work Ethic
- Time Management
- Networking
- Organizational Skills
- Listening

We can add *financial literacy* to the list, and that's where this book comes in.

How many of us can say that we learned these life skills in school? Most will admit that – if they are proficient in any of these areas – it was learned outside of school, and usually learned on the job. The point is: skills differ from knowledge. A student can be in the top of her class in grades and yet be totally unable to carry on an intelligent conversation with an adult, or be unable to balance a chequebook. There are millions of people out of work in the global job market, and our kids are coming out of high school without the necessary skills for making it in the real world.

As you read through this book, there may be ideas and conclusions that you disagree with, and that's alright because these are merely my views and my opinions. But you will have to agree with me on one point: you must realize that if you don't provide financial education for your children, they will receive wrong information from the world. If you do not create a plan for your children, someone else will create a plan for them. And the plans of others will not always be the best plans for your child.

Financial education is the starting point for giving young people the foundation that they need.

INTRODUCTION

A World of Instant Communication

We are living in a fascinating and interesting age. Science and technology have transformed the way we live; not only the way we live but also the way we think and the way we perceive the world around us.

A few years ago, people were transfixed at the thought of cell phones that could be carried everywhere and which allowed us to be connected with other people around the globe. Cell phones as such are now blasé. Today, if you don't have a smart phone that connects you with the Internet as well as with other people, you are totally out of it.

Today's teenagers have never known a world without instant communication, without the Internet, or without cell phones (or some type of hand-held device). They tend to get their information, as well as their socialization, from the Internet.

This generation of children is not spending as much time in quality playtime as their parents did, but rather are mesmerized by playing games on their smart phones. Toy companies can vouch for this change.

Preschoolers Make Buying Decisions

By the time this generation of children reaches the age of three or four, they are already being asked by parents what their choices are when it comes to making purchases. These pre-schoolers know what they want at the fast-food restaurant, they know what they want at the toy counter, and they know what flavour of ice cream they want at the ice cream shop. When their grandparents were that age they were told that children were to be *seen and not heard*. How times have changed.

Teens Spend Billions

Statistics for 2012 show that the dollar amount spent in the US on items by and for teens amounted to a whopping $208.7 Billion.[1] (That's billion with a capital *"B"*)

With all this money, what are these teenagers buying? Top of the lists of teen purchases are:

- Clothes

- Shoes

- Food

- Movies and concerts

- Petrol

Where does the money come from that these teens are spending so freely?

- Gifts

- Jobs

- Parent handouts

- Others (such as grandparents or other extended family members)

- Allowance

- Selling things

Teen Spending in the UK

A research company in the UK, *Mintel*, reveals similar patterns.

They found that the top five items purchased by boys in the UK are:[2]

1. £12.8 million – food

2. £12.3 million – video games

3. £10.7 million – saving

4. £6.5 million – magazines and comics

5. £3.7 million – going out

The top five items purchased by girls in the UK are:

1. £11.4 million – food

2. £9.7 million – saving

3. £7.3 million – magazines and comics

4. £6.5 million – appearance

5. £3.9 million – games

When surveyed, UK Teens revealed that they had high expectations for their financial future, but further questioning caused them to admit their understanding of finances was somewhat skewed.

Wendy van den Hende, chief executive of Personal Finance Education Group, a charity promoting personal finance education in UK schools, said, "In many ways [teenagers] are very switched-on and in control. So there is this weird juxtaposition, because they are very interested in money but are not necessarily clued-up about what they can expect in the future.

"All this points to a need for more financial education for children from a very early age, so they can build up their skills and confidence."[3]

Know How to Spend

Teenage girls in Tokyo spend over $2.5 billion annually on clothing alone, which helps drive home the point that excessive teen spending is becoming a global issue.

With all of this discretionary spending cash, and with all of these buying experiences one would tend to think that the younger members of our consumer society are quite astute when it comes to knowing all about money. Sadly that is not true. For many teens today, the most they know about money is how to spend it. As was stated in the previous quote, teenagers are *not necessarily clued-up about what they can expect in the future.*

Limited Working Knowledge

If this is so, then it would be good to know in what areas they're lacking in financial savvy. In one survey the results showed an extremely limited working knowledge of the following important specifics:

How to manage a credit card – only 35% said they knew how to manage a credit card.

How to balance a chequebook or check the accuracy of a bank statement – 35% were knowledgeable in this area.

How to establish good credit – 38% knew how credit is established.

How credit card interest and fees work – 31% understood these concepts.

What a credit score is – 31% knew what a credit score was.

Whether a cheque cashing service/store is good to use – 25% understood the problems of a check cashing service.

How income taxes work – 22% knew how taxes affected income.

What a pension plan is – 17% (a very small percentage) knew about this most basic savings plan.[4]

I think it would be fair to say that if only 31% of teens know what a credit score is, and the same small percentage are aware of how credit card interest and fees work, then we surely have a great number of young people entering into adulthood at a great disadvantage.

From 1997 to 2010, the financial literacy test scores have fallen nearly 10%.[5]

I see this as an alarming rate. Is it happening because the kids don't want to know? Do they not care? Are they not interested?

Teens Want to Know

That doesn't seem to be the case at all. When asked, teens tell us that they *do* want to know about financial matters.

What do teens most want to know about money? These results may surprise some:[6]

- 74% - How financing works for large purchases such as a car or home

- 72% - Investing money

- 68% - Identity theft

- 62% - Saving money

- 58% - Budgeting

- 55% - Checking accounts

- 55% - Credit cards

Financially Illiterate

For most teens, preparation for adulthood centres on doing well academically (achieving the highest grades possible), and pursuing a field of endeavour such as sports, dance, playing a musical instrument, photography, the arts, and so on. Some students reach university age having played soccer since they were six or seven years old. Many truly become masters in their chosen role.

What a great irony that these same highly intelligent, highly disciplined and gifted students go from high school into the world with such a limited understanding of finances. They are, for all practical purposes, financially illiterate, and therefore are severely handicapped. Most will go on to amass massive credit card debt, or will in some other way sabotage their future by making needless financial mistakes. All of which could be avoided with the correct set of skills.

Missed Opportunities

Parents, as well as schools systems and teachers, seem to be missing a golden opportunity here. Since the largest chunk of money that teens receive is from their parents, it appears that the money is being handed over with little or no instruction, discussion, or guidance in what should be done with the money. For the most part, as I mentioned previously, the most teens know about money is that it is there to spend. Few – very few – understand the concepts of how their money can grow. Few – very few – understand how they can start their own business, and build their own income source(s).

Throughout *Financial Literacy for Teens and Parents,* I will share bits and pieces of my early years—when I was pressed into learning about money as a small child. Through the years, I have been privileged to start thirty businesses. I've travelled the world working with some of the top business minds. None of this happened because I got all the breaks, or because I have the right connections. What I have done to achieve success, I am convinced anyone can do if they have the desire.

My Passion

It's because of my past experiences that I now have a passion to see today's young people have the opportunities to become financially savvy; to become financially literate.

I have designed this book to be read by teens and their parents as a partnership endeavour.

If you are a teen and you have no strong parental presence in your home, I urge you to move forward anyway. I was able to accomplish many things with the help of friends and mentors, and you can too.

If you are a parent of a teen who is not willing to listen or learn, I urge you to read this book anyway. You will glean many ideas, pointers, and strategies to teach and instruct your student even though he or she may not even realize you are teaching.

Four Areas

Four major areas about money will be covered to help to build a strong foundation in financial literacy. They are:

- How to Make Money

- How to Manage Money

- How to Multiply Money

- How to Protect Money

Now what are we waiting for? Let's get started on your journey to financial literacy.

PART I: HOW TO MAKE MONEY

CHAPTER 1: SPENDING MONEY

For teenagers everywhere, below are listed the classic words of advice that are heard from adults, whether that be parents, extended family members, teachers, or counsellors:

- Study hard and get good grades

- Go to university – or some area of higher learning

- Go into a line of work that will be safe and secure

- Hook up with a strong company that will pay a good salary and offer great benefits

- Work hard and earn a decent income to be able to support yourself and your family

- Build up a pension or savings and then retire

And that's it. That's about the sum of all that is taught in life about how to earn a living – or, put another way, how to make money. But is that all? Is that all there is to making money? Study hard and get a job? If it's that simple why are millions of people around the world stuck in a downward spiral of debt and financial problems?

You're thinking *surely there must be more to it than that*. And you would be absolutely correct. There is more to making money, and it begins with a foundation of understanding money, gaining knowledge of money, and becoming comfortable with money.

As was mentioned in the introduction, money is a huge issue in the lives of teenagers, but the extent of their knowledge is limited to how to spend it. Spending money can be likened to the tip of the proverbial iceberg. The act of buying things with your money is but a small fraction of what money is all about.

Why Do We Spend Money?

Spending money happens because each of us *wants* something – or because we *need* something. (Most often, it's the former rather than the latter. This is especially true in the lives of students.) We want something because we either a) see it advertised, or b) see that someone else has that certain item. The way it is advertised, the way it is presented, creates a desire in us to have one as well. It may be the latest smart phone, or the latest name-brand fashions, or to attend a movie or concert.

Young people with a limited understanding of the power of money will be easily swayed by these outside forces. Their wants and desires are determined by the fact that *everyone else has one,* or *everyone else is doing it.* Advertisers are well aware of this pattern of behaviour and they are willing to spend millions of dollars in advertising to present their products to society's younger set of consumers.

My First Experiences with Money

I was born in a village forty miles from Kampala, the capital city of Uganda, in the Luwero District at a time when what came to be called the *Bush Wars* was in full force. The full brunt of these wars was felt in our district, so from a very young age, I was introduced to killing, suffering, danger, and fear. The ongoing wars forced us to move often for the sake of safety.

I was lucky in that I had to learn how to make a profit at a very early age. One of the first things I learned about money was that we could buy items wholesale and sell them retail and thereby earn a profit. However, as you might imagine there were no designer clothes or movies on which to spend the money. Any profit made was spent to purchase food so that we could exist from one day to the next.

None of the profits we earned was mine to keep; it belonged to the family. Money was spent for our basic needs, with none left over for our *wants*. Even though the circumstances in my life were very different from those of most young people growing up today, still and yet, I was learning many basic principles about money.

The point is that much of current teen spending goes on things that in a few months, or even a few days will be forgotten. Little of what is purchased will be of lasting value.

Moses' Family

Sixteen-year-old Moses lives in the UK and comes from a fairly well-to-do family. Both of his parents are professionals who pull in a good income. Moses and his younger sister, Karol, are given weekly allowances for spending money. If there is something extra they want, they simply ask for the money and will nearly always receive what they ask for.

Moses' mother wasn't so lucky growing up, and now she wants to make sure her children have a fun childhood with no *money worries* as she calls it. She says, "If we can afford it, why shouldn't they have what they want?"

As a result, Moses' and Karol's rooms are filled with a plethora of *things* as well as the latest fashions hanging in their closets. They attend the best summer camps and both are involved in sports.

While these siblings are enjoying all the perks of a carefree youth, they have such a limited knowledge of how a household operates, how a budget is set up, how credit works, and how money can grow, that they are headed for a rocky future.

Roy's Family

Roy is fourteen and is the eldest of three younger siblings. Roy's household is a bit different from Moses'. While Roy's parents are not wealthy, they do have an ample income. From his earliest memories, Roy has been called upon to help with the household chores. He and his siblings have a small allowance for necessities such as their lunches and school supplies. Any extra cash needed outside of the necessities, they are required to earn on their own.

This has propelled Roy to be creative about ways to earn money. His parents are willing to pay him for work he does around the house, but for the most part, he does odd jobs for people in his neighbourhood.

Because there is not an excess of money at his disposal, his shopping is highly selective. If there's something he wants, he shops around for bargain prices. Quite often, he shops online on e-Bay and at the bargain shops around town.

At intervals, Roy's parents call a family meeting to discuss the family budget. Roy and his younger siblings have a clear understanding of exactly how much money is earned and how that money is spent. They understand that the mortgage payments, utility payments, groceries, insurance and so on must be paid each month.

The family also discusses upcoming family events such as a vacation, or extra expenses such as for music lessons and sports equipment. This way everyone can pitch in, and each member of the family has a grasp on why certain things must be put off, or rejected altogether.

Your Spending Habits

Nearly everything that has to do with the way we spend money is learned at an early age, and most of our money literacy is learned from our immediate family — usually from our parents. For better or for worse, we establish deep-seated spending habits and ingrained behaviours that tend to follow us into our adult years.

For this reason, it is important to learn as much about money as possible as early as possible. It's much easier to change behaviour as a young person than it will be when you're an adult. When wise spending habits are formed in childhood, they will serve you well throughout your life.

Spending Patterns

Hopefully, you are reading this book because you have a hunger to know how money works and how you can become of the master of your money. You want to develop wise spending habits. The first step is to realize that spending money is guided by ingrained – mostly subconscious – habits; the way to change those habits is to become aware of how and when and under what circumstances the spending happens.

If you are in your room right now, take a good look around. What in your room have you purchased with your own spending money? Take paper and pencil and make a list. It doesn't have to be a complete list. This little experiment is to raise your *spending awareness*.

Spend a few minutes and carefully look over your list.

- If you feel you made a well-thought-out purchase and received good value for the money spent, place a star beside the item on the list.

- If you feel you paid too much, but you still like and want the item and are glad you have it, place a black X beside that item on the list.

- If you wish you had never purchased the item, feel that even a penny would have been too much to have paid, and you're disgusted at yourself for buying it, place a frowning face beside the item on the list.

How did you fare? If you have a bunch of frowning faces, you may want to begin re-thinking about how you spend money.

If there are more black Xs, you may want to learn more about comparison shopping.

If you have mostly stars, congratulations! You're on your way to becoming a wise and thoughtful consumer.

Personality Plays a Part

Another aspect of spending that needs to be taken into consideration is your own distinct personality. While it's true that your family experiences will play a large part in how your spending habits are formed, your personality will also play a part.

Margo and Carmen are sisters who grew up in a household where their alcoholic father was both verbally and physically abusive. Because of his drinking, the girls and their mother were often without money for food. Margo, the older of the two, is more strong willed and outgoing. She is a real take-control person. In her adult years, she became a successful business woman, but lived in fear of never having enough. Her money habits bordered on hoarding.

Carmen, on the other hand, grew up with a *victim mentality* believing that everyone was against her. She saw herself as a loser and blamed people and circumstances for the fact that she could never hold down a job. She maxed out her credits card on splurge spending, rationalizing that she *deserved* the things she bought because she had had such a wretched life. It was impossible for Carmen to watch the shopping channel without buying at least two or three items at a time.

While these two sisters grew up in the same environment, their personalities played a big role in how they were affected and how they dealt with finances. Likewise your personality will play a part in how you manage your spending.

Spending Quiz

Take a minute to take an honest look at how you spend money. Answer the questions below to learn more about yourself and your spending patterns. Remember, this is not a quiz with right or wrong answers. This is why it's crucial to be as honest as possible. The more you know about yourself, the better you will become at taking advantage of your strengths.

Place a tick by the statements that best describe you and your spending patterns:

[ ] I shop mostly for things I absolutely need

[   ] I shop mostly for non-essentials such as clothes, movies, snacks, and music

[   ] I purchase things on sale even if it's something I don't really need or want

[   ] I have a weakness for the latest gadgets – they all look so neat

[ ] I spend more money when I'm out with my friends – if they're spending, it makes me want to spend as well

[ ] I'm able to wait for something I truly want – I save up for it and then I comparison shop for the best value

[ ] I know I should save some of my money, but I never seem to be able to – and it bothers me

[ ] I borrow money from my friends, but never seem to be able to pay it back

[ ] I spend money when I'm unhappy – it works to cheer me up

[ ] I hate to let go of my money – I hang on to what I have

How did you do? Are you seeing how your personality affects how you spend? Think about your life as an adult. Will you be the person who maxes out credit cards and can't pay them off? (More about credit cards later in the book.) Or will you be the person who when things go badly, you run to the mall and buy five new outfits? Is your spending easily influenced by those around you? If and when you get married, how will your spending habits affect the relationship?

Use this new knowledge you now have about yourself to monitor your next shopping trip. Stop and think what is motivating you to make a certain purchase. Is it purely emotional? Or are you making a wise and rational decision? For many this kind of awareness can be a sobering eye-opener.

Spending Affects Everything

Why does the very first chapter of a book on financial literacy start out in a discussion about spending? Because the way you spend money will affect all other aspects of the money matters in your life.

It's a mistaken idea among teens that money will solve problems. This is absolutely not true, and believing this myth will lead to great disillusionment. It's a proven fact that many entertainers and sports figures who pull in high-figure incomes find themselves hopelessly bogged down in debt.

In the same way, individuals who have won a lottery, a few years later find they are worse off than if they had never had the money in the first place. Because they were not sufficiently prepared for such a windfall, they were a pushover for anyone who either asked for a handout, or those who had a great idea for an investment, i.e. scam artists.

While on the surface it would seem that having all that money would be the end of all their worries, for many it was just the beginning of money nightmares. It wasn't the money that caused the trouble – it was the wrong spending habits of those to whom the money came. Had they possessed the insight and wisdom of how to put that money to work, how to curb their spending, and how to protect that money, not only would they have been set for life, but they would have become a positive contributor to their own family and to their community at large.

Now that you have a better understand of exactly how your spending habits affect your life, in the next chapter we'll look at ways you can earn your own money.

CHAPTER 2: EARNING MONEY

Life for most people in the real world consists of a 40-hour week, 40 weeks a year for 40 years. That's how it works. Some of the most successful people in the world worked as teenagers to prepare themselves for the real world. This means they had a head start. You can do the same. But before we begin our discussion on earning, let's look at the various types of income. Most young people think *only* of a job where you work certain hours and get a pay-cheque. But that's not all. Here are three different types of income:

1. Earned income – when you work for money.

    This is the type of income that nearly everyone is familiar with. It can be referred to as trading hours for pounds. This is the way most people first start earning money.

2. Passive income - when money works for you.

    Passive income is money that comes to you for which you do not invest hours of labour; for instance a person who owns a rental property. Work may have been put into the property at the outset, but then the rental income comes every month. This can also refer to an online business where income comes in on a regular basis without a big investment of time. (There are many other examples, but you get the idea.)

3. Portfolio income – again when money is working for you.

    A portfolio refers to investments such as stocks and bonds. As these investments grow, interest is earned. It can then turn into compound interest as you begin to earn interest on the interest.

Understanding the different types of income should be the foundation upon which you begin to build your financial literacy.

Control What You Have

The process of earning money is not always as it appears on the surface. In Chapter 1, we looked at the standard advice most young people hear from adults— study hard, get good grades, get a good job. Earn a salary and so on. This age-old formula is limited in scope. As we have learned, it does little good to earn a great salary if your spending habits are going to eat up all your pay-cheque.

One aspect of earning money has nothing to do with working, or with a job, or with a pay-cheque. It has to do with your *respect* for money. One way to *earn* money is to respect and be in control of what you have.

- How often do you let your money go through the laundry just because you weren't careful enough to check your pockets?

- Do you often lose money because you don't keep track of it?

- Are you quick to give money away to a friend who needs an extra buck and you happen to have one? (While giving is a good thing, it's not wise to give handouts to a habitual moocher. Your money should be more important than that. If you want to give, choose a deserving charitable organization.)

- Is there loose change lying around in your room?

- Do you bother to count the change returned to you after you make a purchase?

I know. You're probably rolling your eyes, and shaking your head. You're thinking that these are such small actions, they don't even matter. But they do matter because small actions lead to ingrained habits, and those habits lead to bigger actions. One day you will have a bank account that will need to be reconciled each month. If you are still careless with your money, that reconciliation may never happen. Errors you may have made might not get discovered until it's too late and you are overdrawn on your account.

If you have never thought about your *money attitude*, now is the perfect time to begin. For a week, watch to see how you respect or disrespect the money that you possess. Realize that if five pounds doesn't matter to you today – it got soaked in the laundry – tomorrow fifty pounds won't matter either. The pattern of disrespect will grow.

Believe it or not, you truly do *earn* the money that you respect. It will stay with you longer and do more for you. View money as your needed tool. Learn to use that tool wisely and skilfully.

Money Earning Possibilities

While many young people receive a regular allowance, and receive money as gifts such as for holidays and birthdays, this chapter is not about those sources. This discussion focuses in on outside sources of income.

When it comes to earning your own money as a teenager, you have a number of options. The first that most think of is a part-time job, but there are other options as well. Keep an open mind, use your imagination, and think big.

- Part-time job

- Offering a service (car washing, dog walking, garage cleaning, lawn work, etc.)

- Selling things

- Serving as an apprentice or an intern

- Making money online

Part-Time Job

Working at a part-time job is a great place to begin your employment experience. Ninety percent of the wealthiest people started out working part-time as teenagers.

The age you must be to apply for a part-time job will vary from one country to another, as does the number of hours you will be allowed to work each week. There are also rules against minors working on a job that may be potentially dangerous. Be sure you know and understand the laws in your country before you start looking.

At the outset, most teens aren't picky. Just a job – any job – is the driving force. There's nothing wrong with this, but it won't take very many jobs to let you quickly know what you like and what you don't like. (In

Chapter 3 I share my experience of working as a mechanic out on the streets. I learned right away that I disliked being dirty and wet.)

Below are a few ideas of where you can begin to place your application.

- Sales clerk in a retail store

- Cinema employee

- Fast food restaurant

- Restaurant waiter

- Shelf stacker in a supermarket

- Warehouse worker

Your first jobs will give you the opportunity to build your reputation as a hard worker—a worker who can be trusted, who can be counted on to show up on time, and who will go above and beyond what is required.

Employers often complain that while young people say they want a job, what they really want is a pay-cheque without putting in any extra effort. Because that is generally true, here is your chance to shine. Because you're ready to go the extra mile, you'll prove yourself valuable to the business and to your employer. Be a person of your word and you will become trustworthy;

become trustworthy and you will never have trouble finding a job.

With your first job, realize that this will be the beginning of your resume. As the years pass, your resume will grow, and hopefully one day it will be filled with great recommendations. So begin now to build your sterling reputation.

What Happened to My Pay-Cheque?

Rodney was excited to land his first job at a clothing store in the mall. He liked retail and liked people so the job was a perfect fit. His starting pay was £7.25 an hour. The first week he was able to put in 20 hours and Rodney was looking forward to that pay-cheque of £145.

When that pay-cheque was in his hands and he took a look at the amount he had received, he was in for a rude awakening. "What happened to my pay-cheque?" he wanted to know.

At home, his parents sat him down and explained exactly what had happened. The first amount held out was for taxes. This was unbelievable to Rodney. "I'm too young to have to pay taxes!" Of course this isn't true. If he'd stopped to think, he would have realized that he'd already been paying sales tax (as VAT) on every item he'd ever purchased for years. We all pay taxes in one form or another.

His parents further explained that it's better to have taxes taken from his wages a little at a time than to have to pay the total tax all at once. And the chances were good that he might even receive a refund at the end of the tax year.

The next item withheld was for National Insurance (or "NI"), which is the UK's "social security" tax-in-all-but-name. His parents also showed him their own paycheque stubs to let him see how much was withheld from their wages.

Once the reality had set in, Rodney quickly learned that he would need to budget differently than he'd first thought.

Offering a Service

When you choose the services option, it will be like being self-employed. Instead of having a boss, you will have clients. Instead of adhering to the store's schedule (or the company's) you will create your own hours. Here as well, it is crucial that you become a person of integrity—you do what you say you will do. Additionally, you are willing to add value to any services that you provide. (In the business world, this is known as *under-promise and over-deliver.*)

Start with what you enjoy doing the most. Take what you know, and turn it into an income; you can make money and have fun while you're doing it. This is definitely an area where your imagination can soar. The sky is the limit. In this busy society we live in, people need things done for them. They need the dogs walked and the flower beds weeded. They need the garage cleaned and the car washed. What can you do best? What are you willing to do? Below are some idea starters.

- Babysitting

- Dog walking (or dog sitting)

- Web or graphic designer

- Blogger

- Garden work (mowing, edging, trimming, weeding…)

- Garage cleaning

- Washing and valeting cars

- Errand boy (This works especially well if you have a bicycle or a car. Senior citizens often need someone to pick up prescriptions for them.)

- Delivering newspapers

- Golf caddy

- Farm hand

- Tutoring (Are you good at maths? Foreign languages? Grammar? There's a mum who would be willing to pay you to tutor her young children who may be weak in that area.)

- Transfer VHS Tapes to DVDs or Digital Format (Tech savvy teens are offering more and more tech services. Many people have large VHS collections and would be thrilled to have them on DVDs. A small ad on CraigsList or Gumtree for your area would pull in clients.)

- Small Engine Repair (This is a great service offer for those who are good with mechanics. This might include lawn mowers, motor scooters, trimmers, leaf blowers and snow blowers. People get irritated and frustrated when their equipment won't work; they need a local repair person.)

The interesting aspect of working in the service industry is that oftentimes one job will lead to another. For instance, a homeowner has hired you to weed all the flower beds. While there, you notice that the rain gutters are full of leaves. Now you can offer an additional service to clean all their gutters. A babysitting job may lead to helping with some of the light housework. And the list goes on. For the young person with an eye focused on possible opportunities, there will always be work.

Selling Things

Are you skilled in the ability to influence the opinions and actions of others? Can you spot a sales opportunity? Do you have a cool head in a negotiation setting? If so, you may have the basic attributes needed to be a salesperson.

However, even for individuals who may not exhibit these traits, it is not difficult to learn the ins and outs of selling. Learning how to buy low and sell high (or buy wholesale and sell retail) is something that can create a good income. Did you know that selling is one of the highest-paying jobs in the world? Another great thing about selling is the salespeople never lack in jobs or opportunities.

Many teens today have set up their own businesses online using the likes of eBay and Amazon; they have learned how to buy pound-shop items and are selling them online for a nice little profit. (More about starting an eBay business on page 50.)

Car boot sales and other flea markets (perhaps called by a different name in different countries) are everywhere, and they allow any person effectively to rent space and set up a small store. Take a few weekends and browse your local flea markets and see what's selling. Find where you can purchase your merchandise cheaply and then resell on your own stall.

One young man named Peter was interested in marbles and quickly learned that many senior citizens, who played marbles as kids, were avid marble collectors. He and his father drove around to estate sales looking for antique marble collections to buy. Sometimes they could pick them up for mere pocket change.

Once he had a sizeable collection of his own, Peter visited flea markets close to his home and discussed the possibility of renting a booth. As it turned out he was able to co-rent with another vendor who only needed a small space; which worked perfectly for Peter. Soon he had a working knowledge of his product and was able to spot the marbles that collectors were looking for. His little business became a great success.

Serving As an Apprentice or an Intern

Serving as an apprentice or an intern may or may not be a paying position; however, it will nearly always *lead* to a paying position. In the meantime, you will be learning life skills, working skills, and inside information about a field in which you have an avid interest. Here's a possible list of ideas:

- Intern at a local museum

- Intern at the zoo

- Intern at a veterinarian clinic

- Intern at the animal shelter

- Intern at the library

- Intern at the paediatric department of the hospital

- Intern in a business setting

Don't take these too literally; they're just ideas to get you thinking.

How to Find Internships

You may have the desire to serve as an intern, but where does one begin? The first and best place is online. Do an online search for internships in your community. You may be surprised what comes up. Request information about what is required to apply. Get the forms or applications needed and start filling them out and turning them in.

In addition to your online search, get the word out to adults that you know. This may include your parent's friends and work associates; your parish priest, a school counsellor, or even your next-door neighbour. Once people know you are looking, and they know your area of interest, the networking will begin.

If there is a specific company that interests you – such as in manufacturing – search their website to see if internships are available. Also, don't be timid about making a few phone calls. Companies are always on the lookout for eager young people who show an interest in their business.

Your willingness to work a few months for free during one summer break could result in a paid position the following summer. This willingness also shows those around you that you are comfortable with delayed gratification (a virtue that is somewhat rare in today's youth). This makes you stand out from your peers and takes you miles down the road of achieving your dreams and goals.

Selecting a Mentor

The subjects of apprentice and intern are closely related to working alongside a mentor. First, what exactly is a mentor? A mentor will be an older person who has extensive experience in the field or industry of interest. Let's say you have a desire to become a veterinarian. The veterinarian you've been taking your dog to for years is someone you admire and respect, but you've never sat down and chatted with him one-on-one. It's usually a quick hello/goodbye as you take the dog in and pick him up again.

Perhaps this is the individual who could pour into your life and answer your many questions about exactly what it takes to make it through veterinarian school (which is very demanding, by the way.) Approach him by asking if he would mind giving you after-hours time during which you could ask him questions and listen to his knowledge.

Realize that this may or may not be a good fit (because sometimes personalities can clash.) Don't be discouraged if this is so; you've taken a first step and you can keep on searching if this is not the right person.

No matter where your interests lie, there is someone who is proficient in that field and who may be more than willing to spend time with you on a regular basis. As it will turn out, the mentor you choose will not only guide you in your career field of interest, but will at the same time impart his or her wisdom in making the right life choices in many other areas.

One mentor suggested to his young protégé, Liam, who wanted to be a chemical engineer, that he drop all sports during his junior and senior years of high school and concentrate solely on getting the best grades possible. "You'll have plenty of time for sports in university," his mentor told him. "After all, you're not seeking a sports scholarship."

Since Liam had a passion for football, it was a difficult decision. After thinking it over, he chose to respect his mentor's opinion. Years later, Liam would say over and over again what a wise decision that had been in his young life. It enabled him to graduate high school with honours, and he walked into a academic scholarship.

The scholarship meant he came out of university with no university loan debt.

(As an added note, whenever you *avoid* going into debt, you are *earning money*. More about debt in Part II.)

Liam and his mentor became lifelong friends, which is what often happens in such situations. Unlike a *life coach*, a true mentor doesn't charge you an hourly fee to advise you. There's nothing wrong with a life coach, because they can be quite valuable, but realize that they are totally different from a mentor.

I think you're getting the picture here. If you do decide that you'd like to enter into an apprentice or internship position, it could be that you will find your mentor in that setting. Keep your eyes and ears open.

A Parent/Teen eBay Business

The wonderful world of eBay commerce presents a great opportunity for your teenager to make her first foray into the world of buying and selling for a profit. Working together will open up an avenue of dialogue and will create a close working relationship. Here are some suggestions on how to get going with your new business:

1. Will you need a business license? Check with your local government to find the answer. Even if a license is not needed, go ahead and give your business a snappy name. It will feel more official that way.

2. The eBay site offers a number of tutorials on their site. Start here: http://pages.ebay.com/education/gettingstarted/registration.html Most of the instructions are basic and easy to understand, but go over them as a precautionary measure.

3. Now go to the post office and pick up a few flat-rate boxes. You want to be prepared ahead of time to ship merchandise as soon as an order comes in.

4. What are you going to sell? What are you interested in? Keep in mind you will be shipping... so choose items that are small, easy to ship, and don't weigh a ton. If you're not yet sure what you will sell, then go to the next step.

5. Spend at least two full weekends at car boot sales, jumble sales, and discount stores. As you browse the dusty, musty aisles you will find that ideas will come to you. Teenagers seem to have a knack for beaming in on what's cool and desirable. One young lady was fascinated with antique broaches – the gaudy, "bling" kinds that women wore in the 1950s. Then she learned

that craft artisans used old broaches to make other jewellery such as necklaces and earrings. Once she decided on her niche, her search was narrowed.

6. The next step is to purchase your initial inventory. Begin small. Don't fill the whole house or the garage. Follow a tight budget and decide ahead of time that you won't pay more than a certain amount for any item. Set your own price parameters. Remember you're in this to make a profit. Also keep in mind that you want your items to fit in the flat rate mailing containers.

7. Time to list on eBay. Learn to create easy-to-read listings with great photos and vivid descriptions. List for at least a week. Start your prices at less than one pound. List with the shipping rate to be added.

8. When the week is over, it's time to take stock of the activity. What sold? What didn't? Can you now narrow your focus? Don't worry about the items that lost money. You're in this to learn, and even losing money can be a learning experience. Of those items that sold, can you get more of those at the same price – or even less? This is how your business will build.

9. Go back to step five and repeat. Find your merchandise on the weekends and sell during the week.

10. Keep a profit and loss sheet. How much does it cost you to travel and buy merchandise? Once you make friends with the vendors in certain flea markets, and they know what you're looking for, they may be willing to work with you and hold back the items you need. This will make your trips more profitable. As you make a profit, determine how much will be reinvested in the business. Decide ahead of time how big you want to grow. You want this to be a fun venture rather than something that consumes your lives.

This plan has worked for teens around the world, and the possibilities are endless. It all depends on where your interests lie. Some teens are more driven than others, some are more organized. However, it doesn't take a whole lot of drive and motivation to make an eBay business happen. The best part is that it requires very little capital to get started, and it can be stopped (or paused) at any time. The flexibility is one of the great benefits—next to the profitability, that is.

What kind of work are you suited to?

The people who are the most successful in life are those who enjoy what they do. They are more likely to be good in their chosen field because it's their passion. In order to follow your passion, you need to ask serious questions:

- What is my favorite subject in school?
- What do I love to do most as a pastime or hobby?
- What are my strong points? (Such as willing to work hard, or having a joyful outlook on life, or being an encourager of others.)
- What are my weaknesses? (Such as not being able to stand up for myself.)
- What talents and skills do I possess now at this time in my life?
- What talents and skills do I most want to sharpen?
- Would I rather work alone or with a group?
- Would I prefer to work inside or outside?
- What kinds of jobs would I hate to do?
- What kinds of jobs would I enjoy doing?
- What can I see myself doing as an adult as a career choice?

CHAPTER 3: CHECKING OUT THE BANK

My First Banking Experience

When I was about nine years old, I became restless and frustrated living in our small village. I wanted more. I wasn't sure what that *more* consisted of, but I knew I had to leave. One night I crawled up on a truck that was going to the nearest town which was the capital city of Kampala. I knew my uncle and cousin lived there; and I also knew my uncle, who was a mechanic, happened to work on the very truck on which I was riding.

Once I arrived I began helping my uncle with his mechanic business. I went to great lengths to make myself very useful. I soon gained his trust, but again I was restless. Working in the grease, and lying underneath a car when it was raining, was not my idea of a good time.

I then connected with a young man who had a small shop that sold cosmetics to women, and I began to help him. (Actually our *shop* was a few shelves in a building with other merchants.) Again, by making myself as useful as I possibly could I earned my right to stay with this young man.

Right away I could see that I needed to have the skill of knowing how to count money. Not only know how to do it, but to count it out very quickly. As it happened, in close proximity to our shop was a bank. Even though I had had no dealings with a bank, I realized that the people there would know how to count money quickly.

I went inside the bank and began to hang around watching the tellers as they counted money out to people. One of the ladies asked what I was doing—why was I just standing there watching? I explained that I needed to know how to count money and to do it as quickly as they did. She was kind enough to take a few minutes and show me a few tricks, such as wetting your fingers as you count so the notes will separate.

That night I practiced with the pages of a book until I could make my fingers fly. The next day I surprised my business associate with my new skill. This made me all the more useful to him in this business.

That little incident was my first introduction to a bank. It certainly wouldn't be my last. Over the years I have come to a greater understanding of what banks and banking are all about; how they can be a help and how they can be a hindrance.

The Money Store

Young people that I speak to as I travel around the world have a limited working knowledge of what a bank does and the part it plays in society's economic picture. Most see it as a very boring place where their parents conduct business. What business it is, they aren't really sure. All they know is it had to do with getting money. (Most aren't really sure how the money gets there in the first place.)

The basic premise of a bank is really not much different from that of a regular store. Think of any store where you shop. Let's say it's an electronics store. How do they stock their shelves? They purchase from a company that manufactures the gadgets. Those companies then ship the merchandise to the store where the employees put them on the shelves. In order to make a profit, the store buys the items at one price, and sells for a higher price. The difference between the two is their profit. For instance they may sell a personal CD player for £30, and they may buy them by the caseloads for £10 each or less.   From the profits earned, the store must now pay for the rent, utilities, employee salaries, insurance, advertising, and so on.

How Banks Make a Profit

A bank is similar to a store except their product is money. They make a profit by borrowing money from people, and then lending money to others. The key is to charge more for lending, and pay less for borrowing.

When your parents and all the other customers of the bank place their money in their bank accounts, that money is then used by the bank to loan out to other entities. Sometimes the bank will make loans to individuals (perhaps to purchase a car or a home); sometimes they make loans to companies (perhaps to start a business, or to upgrade an existing business).

Money is made for the bank when they charge *interest* on the loans. (More about interest in Part III.) Your parents may earn 1 – 2 percent interest on the money they have in the bank. But if they were to borrow money instead, perhaps to buy a new car, then – depending on their credit rating – they may have to pay 3 or 4 percent interest or more.

Because most loans are paid back over a very long period of time, the buyer ends up paying a lot of money in interest. The fees and interest that the bank collects is what keeps the banks in business. As with the store we used as an example earlier, banks use their profits to pay for all of the overhead, plus the salaries of the employees, and to make new investments.

A Typical Banking Account

Most families maintain a typical bank current account. The account holder receives a pay-cheque from his employer and he deposits that money into his current account. Now that the money is in the account, the account holder can write a cheque against that amount.

If the amount of cheques written comes to more than what is in the account, the account is said to be *overdrawn*. That cheque is an *overdraft*. The bank charges a fine for the account holder being overdrawn, and if too many cheques are overdrawn then the fees can mount up in a hurry.

The cheques that are not covered will return to the entity to which it was paid. Some people call this a *bounced check* because it comes back from the bank with the statement *insufficient funds*. Let's say the cheques were written to the supermarket, the electric company, and the rent. Those entities to whom the check were written thought they had been paid, but now have the rude jolt that they haven't been paid at all. It gives you a bad name and that entity may no longer accept your cheques.

Having a current account is a serious responsibility. It's critical that the account be *reconciled* each time the monthly bank statement arrives. Reconciling the account means that your records and the bank's records agree to the penny.

In this era of extensive technology, some people have their pay-cheques automatically (electronically) deposited in their bank account. Also, many households today pay their bills online without ever having to write a cheque. Even so, whether electronically, or by making a physical deposit and writing physical cheques, it's still important not to overdraw on the account.

Are Banks Good or Bad?

Notice if you will that in most towns and cities, the bank buildings are usually the nicest and most up-to-date buildings. Banks are known for making a great deal of money.

So are banks good or bad? The answer is neither and both. They are definitely necessary in the whole scheme of things in the economic world. Your grandparents (perhaps great-grandparents) may not have trusted banks. They may have preferred to hide their money in a jar in the top shelf of the closet; or under the mattress on the bed; or in a coffee can in the basement. Those who lived through war years, or through difficult economic downturns, may have good reason not to trust banks. They may have experienced a bank closing and the consequent loss of all their savings.

If a bank closes today, and some still do, it is usually taken over by another bank. In any case, your deposits are usually protected up to a certain level.

In this day and age, having a bank account (whether a savings account or current account) is a wise step to take. Setting up a savings account will offer you a place to put your money where you will not be as tempted to spend it. (More about saving in Part II.)

Hopefully this chapter about banks and banking gave you more insight into exactly how the banking system works. Now it's time to hand this book over to your parents, because this next chapter is addressed to them. (You can take a little break.)

CHAPTER 4: NOTE TO PARENTS ON "THE TALK"

Dreading "The Talk"

Strange as it may seem, many parents are reluctant to talk openly to their kids about finances. It rates right up there with the dread of having the "birds and bees" discussion. Why this is true is not really clear. It could be due to embarrassment. Some parents aren't all that proud of the state of their own finances and aren't happy about having to air their dirty laundry, so to speak.

Or it may be because the parent simply doesn't realize the need for such openness. They are unaware of the importance of imparting such knowledge. Still other parents are set on allowing their children to just be children and not have them be concerned with the adult world of money and spending.

As for me, I don't even remember being a child in the normal sense of the term since I began working from age nine. I know it's very different for my two daughters. Still, I make it a point to talk to them often about money matters. They know I'm serious about this subject and I will never stop talking to them about their financial future. When I do, I address them as adults because I want them to be able to take responsibility for their own lives. All we can do as parents is to equip them as much as possible while they are young.

The Subtle Overtones

The fact of the matter is, all of us, as parents, are now and have been for many years, teaching our children about money. Perhaps not overtly, but through all the subtle overtones of a normal household, they are catching nuances and meanings.

They may hear us groaning over the pile of bills lying on the desk. Or they overhear heated discussions between parents about who shouldn't have purchased this or that because we *absolutely cannot afford it*. Or they hear talks about a possible layoff at the workplace. Or they ask for an allowance and they are told it's just not in the budget. Or the family holiday has to be delayed until next year – again.

Perhaps your situation is more like Moses' family described in Chapter 1. There's plenty of money, no worries, so you simply see no need to burden your kids with all the details.

Money Covers a Wide Range

The amount of wealth a family has, or does not have, should not be the determining factor of whether or not to have open discussions about money. Stop and think for a moment of all the family ramifications that are directly, or indirectly, related to money and money problems. It covers a wide range. No matter how you look at it, your children are affected.

When our teenagers leave home for university or they start living on their own, how prepared will they be to set up a budget, to live within their means, to spend wisely and not dive so deeply into debt that it will wreck their lives? There are few if any schools that teach the ins and outs of money and money management, so it truly does depend on parents to fill this role.

The stronger the foundation of financial literacy that can be built when they are young; the stronger their financial stability will be when they are on their own.

The learning can begin with something as simple as a family meeting where you and your spouse lay out the family monthly budget. Do they know how much it costs just to keep the power on? How much the mortgage payments are?

Do they know how much it costs for medical insurance, car insurance, life insurance, and property insurance? It has probably never occurred to them before now. But when they purchase their own car one day, they'll need to know how to purchase the insurance and what it might cost.

Young people who are trusted with this kind of information will, first of all, feel a sense of maturity to have been included. Secondly, they will be much more understanding and empathetic regarding what the family can and cannot afford in the way of extras – such as soccer uniforms and sports equipment for instance.

Time to Be Honest

If you have erred into the area of overextending with credit cards – again – it's time to be honest and explain the problem. You may be surprised at how understanding your kids can be. Show them how excessive the fees and interest are on such cards. Help them to grasp the seriousness of the situation.

Sadly, many teens entering university are deluged with offers to apply for their own credit cards, which present buying temptations that few can resist. The feeling of power that an empty credit card gives can truly become addictive. They need to be aware.

Choose to Become Transparent

They need also to be aware that a person can be highly educated, highly intelligent and very successful in their chosen field, and still be financially illiterate. This is why many professional individuals may have poor spending habits. Just because their income is ample, they simply buy more and more *things* – bigger house, new cars, boats, a summer home, and then they live on the edge of bankruptcy. More money is never the answer for money problems.

As a parent, once you swallow your pride, choose to become transparent and openly discuss money, you have now opened channels of dialogue which may not have existed before. It's usually in the teen years when your son or daughter will begin spending more and more time with their friends, or holed up in their room, or involved in extracurricular activities. Time with family becomes limited. These purposeful money discussions can be a partial solution to that communication breakdown.

It's always wise to begin such discussions early on when they are in their primary school years; however, it's never too late. No matter their age, begin today. Don't put it off. Their financial future is at stake.

The Simulation – A Fun Exercise for Parent and Teen

This is an awareness-building exercise. It works best with a younger teen who still enjoys playing "Let's Pretend". The point is to create a simulated income and expenditures sheet as though your student were living on his or her own.

Begin with the salary. He is holding down a full-time job, albeit a barely-above-minimum-wage job. Figure out how much the weekly pay-cheque will be for a 40-hour work week. Explain how taxes are taken out which will actually reduce the take-home amount. Multiply that amount times four to come up with the monthly amount of income.

Now as you brainstorm together, begin to list (and then subtract) typical monthly expenditures:

- Rent

- Utilities

- Groceries

- Phone

- Car (For the sake of this exercise, we'll say no car payments, but there will be petrol and oil and upkeep.)

- Car insurance (This can be pretty expensive for those under 25 years old, so use a realistic amount. The point is to make this as real as possible.)

- Don't forget all those little necessary toiletry items such as shampoo, soap, deodorant, makeup, etc.

- Unless you plan to bring all the laundry home for mum to do, add the expense of weekly laundry

As this simulation exercise continues to grow, throw a kink in the works by introducing an unexpected expense. You have a flat tyre on the way to work and now have to buy a new tyre. How much will that set you back? Will you have to go without something to buy the new tyre?

Most teens who walk through this exercise are quite surprised at how fast their money will disappear each month. This is an especially sobering realization for those who say they *can't wait to be out on their own.*

PART II: HOW TO MANAGE MONEY

CHAPTER 5: HOW TO SAVE

Saving Has Lost Emphasis

Here's a fact that may surprise you, but it's true. Over the course of your working life, it's highly possible that you will earn over a million pounds. Amazing, right? But what happens to it all? The point isn't how much you earn but rather how much of all that money will you keep? That's the reason for this chapter on managing money.

The act of saving money on a regular basis has lost its emphasis in recent years. When your grandparents were in school, saving money was a habit that seemed natural for both children and adults. In some countries, schools offered a school savings scheme in which the students could be involved. This meant that from a young age, savings was an accepted part of money management.

In those bygone days, when a child or a teenager wanted something, they were encouraged by their parents to *save up for it*. If they had no money there was no purchase. This pattern not only instilled in the student a sense of pride and accomplishment, but also taught discipline and delayed gratification. By the time the item was finally purchased, the student had had time to think about, dream about, and anticipate the event. It was worth the wait.

Even though schools – and even society – no longer place a strong emphasis on saving money, this doesn't mean you can't develop the habit in your own life. If up to this point in your life, having extra money meant you could go spend, now try creating a new habit of saving part of it.

The first step will be to have a designated place for the money you want to set back. At first this will probably be some type of piggy-bank in your room. Decide exactly what percent of money you receive you are willing to add to your home *savings account.*

The best way to break an old habit is to create a new one to take its place. That is exactly what you are doing when you begin to save. If you are a detail-oriented type of person you may want to begin to record the money that comes to you. This might be your allowance, wages from your job or other work, money that your parents give you, and money you receive as gifts.

Now decide how much you want to save. A good starting point might be 10%. Instead of randomly tossing money into a jar, or box, or bank, you will be more accurate and specific. Mum gives you your allowance of ten dollars, and before spending any of it that one dollar goes into the savings account.

This may seem like a small thing to you now, but this is how all good habits begin. You are learning how to keep a set of books, and learning how to discipline yourself to set aside money that you will not touch. The more the account grows, the more in-control, and confident you will feel about yourself.

One of the greatest goals when it comes to handling money is for you to be in control of the money, not for the money to control you. You can do this by saying *No* to your tendency to spend every penny that comes to you. Once this happens you will save yourself a great deal of grief later on in life.

Conner's Story

From the time Conner was little, he recalled his mother going on and on about saving money. For him, it was something he was forced to do. In fact, he distinctly remembers his sixth birthday when his grandmother gave him ten pounds to spend. But Conner saw that money for only one short moment before his mother had tucked it into his savings bank. He was not a happy birthday boy. Before he was twelve, a savings account was set up for him at the local bank where the money now went rather than in the piggy-bank on his dresser.

Because saving money was never Conner's idea, it brought little joy and even less sense of accomplishment. Rather he resented it. In spite of that, deep down, he was pleased to see what his mother now called his *university fund,* steadily growing over the years. However, by the time he turned fourteen, he felt it was time to have a heart-to-heart talk with his mother.

He explained to her that while he was pleased that she wanted him to save, he now felt he was old enough to make buying and saving decisions on his own. He explained that he needed to be learning to take responsibility rather than her doing it for him.

At first, his mum stiffened. She took it personally, thinking Conner meant that he didn't appreciate what she viewed as great training in money management. However, after thinking it over, she realized he was getting old enough to handle his own affairs. Together they hammered out a plan whereby Conner agreed to save a certain percent of all the money that came to him.

It was some time later that Conner was able to tell his mum that he wished she had been a little less stringent in her plan to save all *his* money. There needed to be a balance in the system.

Society Stopped Encouraging Saving

As mentioned earlier, much of the foundational teaching about saving money has gone by the wayside in our present culture. Another way that saving has been discouraged rather than encouraged is the low rate of interest paid on a bank savings account. (More about interest in Part III.) Thirty years ago banks were paying around 9% or 10% interest on savings accounts; today it's closer to 1%. With such low interest payouts much of the overall motivation to save has diminished greatly.

With these two strikes against you – the savings concept not being taught, and banks paying low interest rates – the motivation to save must be something that you decide to do for your own reasons. You must see the need to sock money away; you must see how important it is not to spend every penny that comes into your hands. Hopefully by reading this book, you are beginning to understand the importance and how it will greatly affect your life both now and in the future.

Time to Open Your Account?

At some point, you will graduate past the bank in your room. You will want something safer, and you will want your money a bit further from your temptation to *rob your own bank.* The next step will be your own savings account in an actual bank.

Don't be surprised if the bank doesn't exactly roll out the red carpet for you – even if it's the bank where your parents are customers. Yet another deterrent to young people learning to save is that some banks no longer cater to students as they did in years past.

On a rare occasion you will find a bank that will allow those under the age of eighteen to open your own account, and make deposits and withdrawals on your own. But as I said, that is rare. It's more likely that one of your parents will have to co-sign, or set up a custodial account. If it's the latter, that parent will have to sign before you can make a withdrawal.

Shop around. You don't have to bank at the same bank as your parents. Ask about interest rates, and also ask about fees such as service charges. Yes, it is your money and yes you are helping the bank by having your money there, but at some banks, if your account drops below a certain amount they will tack on a service fee. This can eat up any earned interest in a big hurry.

How easy will it be to make withdrawals? This is important. If you are saving for something special, and it's time to make the purchase, there should be no hassle to get your money out and buy your prized possession.

Once you find the bank you're looking for, you'll need some sort of identification such as a passport or driving licence in the UK, or a social security number in the US (other countries have similar identification numbers). That number will be required as you fill out the forms to create your new account.

How About a Credit Union?

You may have heard of credit unions and building societies before. In fact, your parents may bank with one. These institutions are created by people of a common interest – such as a workplace – and they are owned and operated by the members. Banks, on the other hand, are owned and controlled by their shareholders.

Because credit unions and building societies exist for the welfare of the members, their profits are reinvested into the system. Because of this, these institutions may (but not always) provide loans at lower interest rates. As with banks, your deposits should be protected up to a certain level.

Children and teens may find it easier to open an account with a credit union or building society (or even a bank) if an existing family member already banks there and can "refer" you.

There's a saying that *a penny saved is a penny earned.* No matter if you think the saying is old fashioned, it's as true today as it was in the past. Money that you do not spend is money you have – in essence – earned for yourself.

Pay Yourself First

Paying yourself first – putting an amount of money back – is a marvellous habit to create early in life. It will be a habit that will stand you in good stead for the rest of your life. While you may *think* you will set back a little money when everything else is taken care of, this will seldom happen. The money will be gone and you'll have saved none of it.

Before you ever receive your first pay-cheque, or even when you are beginning to receive an allowance, make sure the first thing you do is to put a certain percent aside as your savings amount. As was mentioned at the beginning of the chapter, having a designated place for your savings will help a great deal. And hopefully, at some point, this will be your own savings account. We will talk in the next chapter about how to set up an actual budget, which will include learning how to *pay yourself first*.

In order to become an excellent money manager, take steps this very day to become a disciplined saver. You'll never regret it.

Be a Wise Shopper

Here are a few tips to help you use wisdom and create good habits when shopping.

Shopping Is Not Entertainment

Hanging out at the shopping mall as a way to be entertained sets up a perfect scenario to see something that you feel you *must* have. Because you see it, you want it. Impulse buying takes over.

Look for Sales

Those items you saw last week and thought you had to have, this week they are on the sale for 30% off. Aren't you glad you waited? Aren't you glad you've learned to look for sales?

It Doesn't Have To Be the Shopping Mall

Once you break the habit of hanging out at the mall, you'll find other places to make your purchases such as discount stores, factory outlets, and consignment and second-hand stores. Many second-hand stores have designer clothes that are as good as new and cost only a fraction of the original price.

Attend Matinees

Just like all your friends hang out at the shopping mall, all your friends probably go to the movies at night. But why? The movie is exactly the same in the afternoon and costs much less.

Another way to save at the movies is to eat before you go, then plan to have pizza afterward. Why pay the jacked-up prices for snacks in the cinema? You're smarter than that.

The Art of Saving

Respecting your money and saving your money are learned arts. It will become rather like a treasure hunt to you. The more you discover ways to save, the more you will *want* to look for ways to save. It can become quite addictive. And what a wonderful addiction to have. It will pay off big time.

CHAPTER 6: "BUDGET" IS NOT A DIRTY WORD

Restrictive and Painful

Why is it that teens often balk at the thought of creating and operating a budget? Is it because it sounds too much like doing their homework? Or it sounds boring? Or perhaps it's because they think that a budget is like wearing a pair of too-tight shoes – restrictive and painful.

Imagine, if you will, a business that had no clue how much money was being spent on their wholesale merchandise, their employee salaries, their advertising, or the rent on their facility. How long would that company be in existence? If you said *not very long,* you'd be one hundred percent correct.

In order for any business to make a profit, in order for them to assess where spending should be cut, or where they can expand, every penny must be accounted for. You would never hear the CEO of a large corporation say to his accounting department, "Please, don't send me the budget reports this week. It's just too restrictive to have to follow all those numbers. We here at QRS

Corp just want to be loose and free." Everyone would wonder if he might need to take an extended holiday. What corporate leader in his right mind would not want to know how much is going out and how much is coming in?

Your Miniature Corporation

It's time for you to think of your finances as a miniature corporation and you are the CEO. You are the chief officer in charge. It's time to take control. The word *manage* actually means to "be in charge of something," and you definitely want to be in charge of your money.

At this time, you may receive an allowance, but sooner or later you will be receiving other income either with a part-time job or through some of the other avenues discussed in Chapter 2. The sooner you become the master of your money the easier it will be. Do it while the amounts are small and you will just naturally progress into managing larger amounts. When it's time to leave for university, or to live on your own, you will be prepared.

What is a Budget?

Another reason teens may rebel at the thought of a budget is that they aren't really sure what it entails. It sounds like a lot of boring bookkeeping. Put in simple terms, a budget is an itemized summary of income and expenses for a given period. For most students, it's not a problem to write down the amount they receive each week, but it's a pain to have to list what is spent. "You mean I have to write down every time I buy a pack of chewing gum? That's insane." Not only is it *not* insane, it will become quite profitable in the end.

Be honest. One pack of chewing gum is seldom purchased alone. It's usually purchased along with a soft drink and a couple of chocolate bars. And yes, it should be written down. At least in the beginning. But we're getting ahead of ourselves.

How to Set it Up

First, decide where your budget will be kept. Will you set it up online? Or will it be in a notebook on the desk in your room? Or will it be a small notepad kept in your backpack or purse? It doesn't matter which you choose but decide what works for you and then stick with it.

You may want to create the actual budget online by using online forms, but then use a smaller notepad to jot down how much you spend each day. You can then easily transfer figures from your notepad over to the online form.

Here's a great example of a workable budget form you can use:

http://www.moneyandstuff.info/pdfs/SampleBudgetforTeens.pdf

You can use this form, or copy the idea using the format that works best for you. (Notice I keep saying "what works for you," because if the process doesn't fit you and your personality, it'll never last past the second week.)

I warn you ahead of time, keeping a budget can become addictive. I see you rolling your eyes. You don't believe me, but it's true. If up until now all your finances have been a blurry hodge-podge – spending who knows how much on who knows what; throwing loose change and banknotes around like a bag of yesterday's stale crisps; wanting something but never knowing if you can afford it – you are going to be very surprised at how much fun it is to take control and bring order to the chaos.

Like a Picture

Your budget will be like a picture that shows you exactly where you are at any given moment. With this clear picture before your eyes, you can more easily see where you are losing cash. Were you actually aware that you spent that much on snacks every week?

One of the first things a budget will show you is – are you operating in the red or in the black? Operating in the red means your outgoings amount to more than your income. This might not matter today, because mum and dad are always there to pitch in and make up the difference. But – news flash – mum and dad are not always going to be right there by your side. In a few short years, you will be out on your own. If you have a shortfall then, will you resort to using a credit card or a payday loan? (More about the dangers of debt in the next chapter.)

Learning to live within your means, not spending more than you have, is one of the foundational principles of money management. Conquer this and you will be a proficient money manager.

Setting Goals

Another thing your budget will do is allow you to begin to set reasonable financial goals. With the figures on the page (or the computer screen) you can see exactly how to take your savings right off the top. You will **be paying yourself first** before any other spending takes place. (See the section on paying yourself first in Chapter 2.) Once that amount is budgeted and set apart, you operate with the balance for other expenditures. When the money is gone you stop spending. Simple.

Everyone is going out for a movie, but you're prepared to say, "Can't do it this week. It's not in my budget." Then put some steel in your backbone and follow through. Believe it, a week or so later when you do have the cash you'll have a better time than if you robbed your savings to go. This is how you will become a conscientious, smart consumer.

Identifying Priorities

Yet another benefit of keeping a budget is that you become aware of the difference between your wants and your needs. You will become aware of what's important to you. It's called identifying priorities.

Mel is a budding ballerina, but her leotards and shoes are quite expensive. She knows her parents sacrifice to pay for her classes, so she wants to help pay for her costumes. This is high on her priority list. She would gladly skip a few movie nights with friends in order to purchase the best pointe shoes.

As you walk through a few months of keeping your budget, you too will discover what is truly important to you and that will guide your buying decisions.

As mentioned, a budget helps in setting goals. For instance, Mel has her heart on attending a two-week advanced summer ballet class. That's one of her short-term goals. It's listed in bold letters on her budget sheet and it motivates her to build up her savings account with that goal in view. To her way of thinking, it's worth any sacrifice she has to make. Additionally, she has a long-term goal of saving for her university tuition. Her budget sheet helps her see exactly where she stands for both of these goals.

A Spending Weakness

Week after week, month after month, your budget will reveal your spending patterns. This can help you to see where you might have a spending weakness. What is it that you can't seem to resist? A daily cappuccino? Another piece of jewellery when your jewellery box is already overflowing? The latest pair of designer jeans?

No matter what it is, if it's causing a dent in your budget then it's an area that needs attention. The first couple of times you resist the temptation may be difficult, but after that you are in control. It's an exhilarating feeling of pride and accomplishment. Share your victory with someone who will understand. Celebrate that victory!

No Two Budgets the Same

Every teenager's budget will vary due to whether or not they receive an allowance, and whether or not they are required by family rules to pay for some of the big-ticket expenses such as clothing, entertainment and school supplies. For this reason there is no such thing as a one-size-fits-all when it comes to creating and keeping a budget. Again, it has to fit your needs and your circumstances.

For the best results, work closely with your parents as your budget is being formulated. Ask for their input and their advice. As they see your level of discipline and dedication, they will be much more willing to trust you with more money and with more spending responsibilities.

You may want to work out an agreement on clothing purchases, which is a major expense for most teenagers. For instance higher priced items such as shoes, winter coats (if you live where it gets cold), and special occasion clothing such as a dress suit for the guys or a prom gown for the girls, are covered by the parents. The smaller items are the responsibility of the teen. If you know the parameters ahead of time, you can then budget accordingly. (Believe it, when the responsibility is on your shoulders, you will learn where the sale racks are in every store!) The best agreement between you and your parents is the one that functions well on an ongoing basis.

Now that you have your budget in place, you can more clearly understand how and why spending can get out of hand. In the next chapter, we'll take a look at how financial disasters happen. The key word is *debt.*

What is Inflation?

You are at Old Navy looking at a pair of jeans. They're just like the ones you bought last year, but now they cost five pounds more. At the cinema tickets have gone up fifty pence. At your favorite coffee shop the price of a cup of cappuccino has gone up as well. What does all of this mean for you and why should you be aware?

When prices go up, buying power goes down. What this means for you is that the money you are saving for university, in five or six years from now will not have the same buying power that it does now.

Let's say you have a part-time job and you hold that job for two years. If you never receive a raise, at the end of the two years, in essence you will be earning *less* because it will not buy as much as it did two years prior. Raises in pay are necessary to keep up with the rising prices.

Inflation is one of the biggest reasons you must understand how to make your money grow.

(More about How to Multiply Money in Part III.)

CHAPTER 7: THE INSIDE SCOOP ON DEBT

There was a great Rihanna concert coming to town. It was the one Carlos had been waiting for. All his friends were going and tickets were selling fast. But there was just one problem – he was short on cash. He had some money tucked away, but not enough to cover a concert ticket. When he counted it up, Carlos discovered he was short fifteen pounds. What to do?

The answer was easy. His buddy, Stephen, always had extra money; his parents were loaded. Carlos was sure Stephen wouldn't mind loaning the money. And he was right. Stephen was willing to pitch in the difference Carlos needed so he was good to go.

The concert was out of sight. Carlos had the time of his life. Afterward when the gang stopped for pizza, since Stephen knew Carlos was strapped he even loaned ten more pounds to pay for the pizza. What a friend.

It was so simple and easy to borrow the money from Stephen, and Carlos felt sure at the time that it would be just as simple and easy to pay back the twenty-five. But it didn't turn out that way. It seemed like things just kept coming up and the money was never there. Now whenever he saw Stephen in the halls at school he felt like a jerk; he wanted to turn around and walk the other direction.

Now picture yet another scenario. Carlos arrived at school one morning to find Stephen at his locker waiting for him and which gave him a sense of panic. Stephen announced that from now on, every week that Carlos didn't pay back the money it would cost him an extra pound per week. So now Carlos' debt is *growing*.

What just happened here? Carlos inadvertently slipped into the trap of easy debt. This happens to people every day in every part of the world. Borrowing money is so easy and at the time it seems like the perfect solution. This is what's known as taking the *path of least resistance.*

What if Carlos had made the difficult decision to just skip this concert? After all, he really couldn't afford to go. Yes, it would have been a bummer for the moment – especially the next day when everyone raved about how much fun they had. But no one is talking about the concert now. It's old news. All his friends are moving on to bigger and better things, while Carlos is still stuck owing Stephen.

We've mentioned this before, but it bears repeating – waiting because of being unable to afford something is known as *delayed gratification.* To be honest, there are adults twice your age who have never learned this concept and they suffer greatly because of it. The sooner you learn how to live with delayed gratification, the more prosperous you will become.

Finally, Carlos turned to his parents and admitted his foolishness. He then asked them for jobs they might give him to do in order to earn the money to pay Stephen back. It turned out well in the end, and Carlos learned a lasting lesson about debt.

My First Encounter with Debt

Through a series of events, I was able to travel from my home country of Uganda to the UK at the young age of fourteen. I was filled with great hope and high expectations. My plan was simple. I would get a job, work for six months, raise enough money to purchase goods and return to Uganda and sell them and double my money. I had been told that a person could come to the UK and make more money than someone who worked in an office in Uganda. It all sounded so promising, but I was in for a rude awakening.

I wasn't used to the cold weather in England, I was all alone, I could speak very little English, and I could find no work. I was miserable. Most of what was available in the way of jobs was manual labour and I was a skinny little kid unable to do such hard work. My money was running out and I was frightened. I wasn't sure what I was going to do.

As if all of this wasn't bad enough I had yet another burden to carry. I had borrowed money from people back home in Uganda who believed in me. They knew what a hard working and determined kid I was. They loaned me the extra money I needed to complete my passport and get my plane ticket. They trusted me explicitly. (The only persons who knew my plans were my nine-year-old brother and my five-year-old sister. This may sound weird, but the only ones I could trust at the time were my younger siblings.) So now I was in debt and going back home empty-handed was not an option. I'll never forget the dreadful feeling deep in the pit of my stomach knowing that I had let these people down. But more importantly I didn't want to let myself down.

As it happened, my good fortune turned around and I was able to pay them back, but that's another story. The fact is that being in debt placed a burden on my young shoulders that made a bad situation a great deal worse. Like Carlos, I learned an important lesson about debt when I was very young.

Types of Debt

The truth is, not all debt is bad. If it were not for certain types of business loans, many companies would never be able to start up or grow. Without loans, people would be unable to purchase cars and houses.

Almost every family who owns a home has a mortgage. This is a debt, but it's not an unwise debt. It's not a speculative or risky debt. (That is, unless you took the loan out for more than the house was worth and then the prices plummeted. Then there would be serious trouble.) For the most part these types of debt are not dangerous, but they can still cause problems.

When you apply for financing to get a loan for a house, this is called a *secured* loan. The loan is secured by the property. The lender knows that if the homeowner defaults on the house, they can still recover their money by taking back the house and selling it.

An *unsecured* loan is a loan that has no collateral as backing. If a person defaults on an unsecured loan the most the lender can do is sue for the money and possibly garnishee that person's wages. Student loans are considered an unsecured loan, as are payday loans and credit card debt.

Understanding a Mortgage

A mortgage is one of the most common debts for a family to undertake, because everyone needs a home to live in. It's true that some families rent, but even then it's usually their goal to one day buy their own home. There's a special feeling of pride and achievement that comes with the purchase of your own home.

You may be thinking that step for you is a long way down the road, and perhaps it is. But today is the best time for you to understand and be aware of the many ramifications of acquiring this huge debt.

The purchase of a home is nearly always the largest purchase most people will ever make. (It's my hope for you that you will have many bigger investments than just your residence.) A home purchase often amounts to tens of thousands of pounds, and more often, hundreds of thousands of pounds.

In earlier generations couples saved their money for many years to put down as large a down-payment on a mortgage as possible. In our present culture, the scene has drastically changed. Now couples – or individuals – when buying a house look for financing that will cover the entire price of the home. This makes for some pretty hefty mortgage payments.

It's important to understand that until the mortgage is paid off, the bank (or the lending company) owns your house. If the payments are not made, the bank can come and take it away.

There are different types of mortgages. It's good to have a working knowledge of how these work and which ones are the most economical. Let's look at the two most common ones.

30-Year Fixed Rate Mortgage:

Monthly payments are lower

Interest rates are higher than with a shorter mortgage

Accumulated interest may be tax-deductible (in the USA)

15-Year Fixed Rate Mortgage:

Monthly payments are larger than with a longer term mortgage

Interest rates are lower

Accumulated interest is lower

Essentially what this means is if you are willing to make larger house payments each month you will save on the interest and the house will be paid off earlier. Here's how this might look:

30-Year Fixed Rate Mortgage:

Loan principal: £100,000

Interest: 8%

Payments: £733.76

Total interest paid: £164,155.25

15-Year Fixed Rate Mortgage:

Loan principal: £100,000

Interest: 7.25%

Payments: £912.86

Total interest paid: £64,315.32

So few homebuyers go into a mortgage situation with this knowledge and yet these figures are staggering. The buyer who chooses a 30-year mortgage at 8% interest will end up paying £264,155.25 for their £100,000 house. At that price they could have purchased two houses.The buyer who chooses the 15-years mortgage and arranges their budget so they can pay the extra couple hundred pounds a month in house payments, will in the end save around *£100,000* in interest. (One hundred thousand pounds is a lot of money in anyone's estimation!) Plus their house will be paid off in half the time. Which would you chose?

Interest rates are always changing, and closing costs and other variables will affect these numbers. In spite of that, no matter how you adjust the numbers, a shorter-term loan will always, without fail, save a massive amount of money.

Homebuyers who go into a mortgage situation armed with this kind of knowledge are planning ahead. The plan might include what will happen once the mortgage is paid off. That extra £900 can then be invested. Perhaps it can be used to purchase another house as an investment property. Or they may invest in a business property that will create passive income. The options are endless. On the other hand, families who are locked into a long-term mortgage are chained to those payments for most of their income-producing years.

Overbuying

Another pitfall in making a house purchase is purchasing a home that is above the buyer's ability to comfortably pay for. It happens all too often that a buyer sees his house as a status symbol. It amounts to wanting what everybody else has—and to have it even better. Very little wisdom goes into a transaction built on such a shaky foundation.

Before beginning to house-shop, it would be smart to sit down and do a few calculations. Will the house payments be based on one salary or two? If two, calculate what might happen if one salary should cease to be. Be realistic and figure out the worst case scenario. Does the amount of the payments allow for other necessary expenses to be covered? Can you still add to your savings or invest for the future? Being *house poor* is no fun. How can the family enjoy a nice house when the large payments mean there's nothing extra to take a vacation now and then?

In spite of the fact that house buying is such a common occurrence, it's defies logic that so few people actually understand the finer points of how a mortgage works. Hopefully, you will be much smarter than many of your elders. Now that you know, you'll make better decisions.

Payday Loans

Payday loans are one of the more dangerous of all the different types of loans. As the name implies it encourages the borrower to come into the loan office and get a *quick loan* just to *last them until payday.* Of course, when payday comes, they need all of that pay-cheque to cover the household bills, and yet the loan is still due and owing. (This is much like the situation of Carlos when he borrowed money to attend a concert.)

You will notice these ads for payday loans on the radio, TV, Internet, and even ad pieces that you receive in the mail. The ads are designed to be compelling and enticing. Nearly always there will be pictures of money with the promise that it will be quick and easy to have a few extra pounds in your pocket.

Here are some of the different names this type of loan goes by:

- Payday loans

- Cash advance loans

- Check advance loans

- Post-dated cheque loans

- Deferred deposit cheque loans

The process goes something like this. The borrower writes a cheque for the amount they need to borrow, plus a fee tacked on. The lender gives the borrower the amount of the cheque less the fee. The lender agrees to hold that check until the borrower's next payday.

If the borrower still cannot pay back the loan, it is rolled over for another week—with an added fee. This can add up to exorbitant rates of interest. It's designed to get the unsuspecting person snared in a web from which they cannot get free. Millions of people get caught in these loans and regret the day they took out that first one.

A better solution is to call your creditors and request more time to pay the bills. There may be a late charge, but it will be small in comparison to the high interest rates of a payday loan.

Pawnshops

Sometimes when people get into a financial bind, they will take something of value – such as jewellery – and pawn it at a pawnshop. The owner of the pawnshop will then give that person cash for the item. Pawning, as it is called, has been around for many years. You have no doubt seen such shops around your hometown as well. Here's basically how it works:

1. You bring in something you own and give it to the pawnbroker as collateral for a loan (this act is called pawning).

2. The pawnbroker loans you money against that collateral.

3. When you repay the loan plus the interest, you get
    your collateral back.

4. If you don't repay the loan, the pawnbroker keeps
    the collateral.

When you pawn your valuables, you may stand to lose
that item, but you are not sucked into high interest rates
as with the payday loans. Eventually, however, you
may run out of valuables to pawn, and this is certainly
not the pathway to financial security.

[As an added note: For those of you involved in an eBay
business as described in Chapter 2, a pawnshop is a
marvellous place to discover bargains to resell. You
never know what you will find there. It's rather like one
big flea market and estate sale all combined.]

Hopefully, through these examples you are catching the
importance of living within your means. No amount of
loans – no matter what the interest rate – will ever make
up for poor spending habits. In fact, poor spending
habits means you will forever be at the mercy of lenders
(or pawnbrokers).

Credit Cards

The discussion of money management is not complete
without the inclusion of the subject of credit cards. The

next chapter will be devoted to the ins and outs, the ups and downs, and the pros and cons of credit cards.

Note to Parents – When to Open a Current Account

By the time your student is in the latter years of high school, and if that student has been working (either part-time or with a summer job), and if that student has proven to be a responsible spender, this would be a good time to open a current account. It's certainly better to set this up while they are still at home, so that you can teach them how to keep track of cheques written and how to reconcile with the bank as soon as the statement arrives in the mail.

It's a sad state of affairs if a young person is learning how to balance a chequebook when he is away at university. One university counsellor recalled when a young female student rushed into his office in a panic. She was waving a handful of cheques in her hand moaning that all of these were *bounced cheques*. It turned out that these were the cancelled checks that the bank routinely returned to their customers; but this poor girl was totally unaware and uninformed.

The Best Bank

When looking for the best bank for a current account for a teenager, you will want to ask a few questions:

- Does this bank pay interest on a basic current account?

- Does this bank require a minimum balance?

- Does this bank charge a monthly fee?

- Does this bank charge for each cheque written over a certain limit?

Look over the choices of accounts offered. Each one will be different in services and costs.

Using a Debit Card?

A debit card can be a quick, hassle-free way to pay for items; however, it can also be an easy way to lose track of spending. You know your student, so only offer a debit card if you're sure he will keep close tabs on every time he pulls out the card for a soft drink at the convenience store.

If and when you decide your student is ready for a current account, sit down and go over every detail from how to make a deposit to how to reconcile the monthly statement. No detail is too minor to be discussed. The more educated they are now, the fewer headaches will come along later.

CHAPTER 8: THE DEEP PIT OF CREDIT CARDS

I was told that back in the 1980s, a funny joke was going around. In fact, it appeared on T-shirts and bumper stickers. It said something to this effect:

"I borrowed from my Visa to pay my MasterCard."

At the time, this was a very funny joke. Today, no one thinks it's so funny, because it's an everyday occurrence. People bounce credit card balances around from one account to another in an attempt to save on the fees and interest. It never solves the problems, but like the payday loans discussed in the previous chapter, it becomes a trap which is difficult to get free from.

Teenagers in today's world cannot imagine life without credit cards. So how did all this plastic stuff begin in the first place? It happened in 1949 when a businessman in New York City went to pay his bill at a restaurant and discovered he didn't have his wallet.

His name was Frank McNamara, and he'd just eaten dinner at New York's Major's Cabin Grill. The bill was brought to the table, and it was at that moment McNamara realized he'd left his wallet at home. While he was able to get out of his current predicament, he began to think there had to be a better way. How could a person pay for something with no cash?

He and his business partner, Ralph Schneider, put their heads together and came up with an idea. The following year, the two men returned to the Major's Cabin Grill and paid the bill with a small, cardboard card. They called it the *Diners Club Card*. At the outset the card was used for travel and entertainment purposes. These early cards were not called *credit cards*, but rather were called *charge cards*. The holders of these cards paid the bill at the end of the month. It would never have occurred to them to let the bill run up month after month.

The idea took off and by 1951, cardholders numbered around 20,000. The cards remained in their cardboard state until ten years later when plastic cards were introduced. And it was in the 1960s that MasterCard and Visa came into being. Now the banks became involved. Instead of paying balances off at the end of each month, these newer credit cards allowed the holders to pay minimum payments on the balance and carry over the difference to the next month.

Advertising was then ramped up making the possession of a credit card appear to be the *in* thing to do. Eventually, people were making ordinary everyday purchases such as clothing, petrol for the car, and groceries, and were putting them on their credit cards. It was all so *easy*.

One of the most glaring problems of a credit card is that the holder loses sight of actual numbers. Remember when we talked about how a budget allows you to have a *picture* of where you stand with regard to expenses? The credit card does a good job of *hiding* actual expenses. It opens the door to *not* living within your means. The temptation of whipping out a credit card at a moment's notice means there is less chance that you will think over your purchase. Bad buying decisions are far more likely to happen.

Teens and Credit Cards – Heated Controversy

Is it good for a teen to have and use credit cards? Some say yes; some say no. The *yes* side says that this is the best way for teens to learn how a credit card works while they are still under the guidance and supervision of their parent.

The *no* side says that the only way to teach teens good financial habits is with cold, hard cash. This side says that making a purchase with a credit card is too abstract. No cash changes hands, and the reality of the amount of purchase never hits home.

No matter which side you lean toward, the truth is most kids want their own credit card... not so much to make purchases, but simply because they want to look cool in front of their friends. And there is a world of difference between going to the shopping mall with a credit card in your pocket, and going with £20 cash in your pocket. It causes a whole different buying attitude.

Another problem with teenagers, as credit card holders and users, is that they are much more familiar with the buying end than with the paying-off end of the transaction. Remember when we looked at the enormous difference in interest paid on a 30-year mortgage as compared to a 15-year mortgage? The numbers are eye-popping! Let's do the same thing with interest rates on a credit card.

Understanding Credit Card Interest Rates

While many card holders shop around for the lowest interest rates for the card they want to use, few are aware of how the monthly interest fees are calculated. The sad fact is that the credit card companies are counting on the fact that no one understands how the rates are calculated.

In Part III, we will learn more about compound interest, but for now just know that with a credit card the power of compound interest is *working against you.*

Let's look at an example:

Let's say you have your own credit card and you have an owing amount of £100 on it. Let's also say that it will accrue 10% interest. (I'm using 10% because it makes it simple to calculate, but most rates are much, much higher.) This means the first month, you will be charged £10.

Now compound interest kicks in. The next month that 10% will be applied to the full £110 amount. Now your interest amounts to £11 so your debt is now £121. Amazing right?

If you are fooled into thinking that the interest will only apply to the original debt month after month, you will be in for a shock.

Furthermore, without getting too technical, some card companies compound on a *daily* basis rather than on a monthly basis. Now the interest really begins to grow.

Before we leave these nightmare scenarios, look at this possibility. Were you aware that if you fail to make your payments on time that the credit card company can – without warning – raise your interest rates? How much that increase amounts to will depend on your particular situation, but it could be sizeable. Now, in spite of the fact that you dutifully shopped for the lowest rate card, you are now faced with compound interest with a higher rate.

Oh, and another thing. As was stated, the reason the rates increased was because payments were not made on time. If payments are not made on time, they charge a late fee. Now the interest applies not only to your debt, and to your interest amount, but also the added-in late fees.

Is your head hurting yet? Now you can see why so many people are literally drowning in credit card debt. The credit card companies make it almost impossible to get free once you are hooked. Believe me, when I say this is not a fun way to live your life. While some teens see a credit card as *magic money* in their pockets, it doesn't take long for the magic to fade when the reality of repayment hits.

It's usually when you turn eighteen, or at the time when you leave for university, that you will be inundated with glittering, hard-to-resist, offers from credit card companies. You are now their prime target. But you are now armed with knowledge. Don't become their victim.

Once you are trapped in credit card debt, you are no longer in control of your finances.

Okay, it's time to hand the book back over to your parents. After this gruelling section on credit cards, you deserve a break! Chapter 9 has to do with allowances for kids – something parents can get confused about. This information could be a big help.

Minimum Payment Credit Card Payoff

> Your credit card has a balance of £5,000. The interest rate is 14%. You make no more purchases on this card. The minimum payment amounts to 2% of the balance. (You're strapped – minimum payments are all you can afford.) If you continue to make only the minimum payments, it would take *22 years* to pay off this balance. And – are you ready for this? – in that 22 years you will have paid *£5,887 in interest.* More than the original purchase amount.
>
> Was that purchase really worth it?

Credit Score / Credit Report

One **of the biggest dangers of using a credit card is getting caught in the snare of building up a debt that becomes nearly impossible to pay off. However, an** even bigger danger is the possibility of damaging your credit rating.

I am continually amazed how few young people are aware that any history of late payments and missed payments are sent to the major credit card reporting agencies. Your poor credit history will follow you for many years to come.

The two major reporting agencies in the UK are Equifax and Experian. It is the role of these agencies to compile and comprise your credit rating. Your credit report consists of the composite of your credit history. This is the information that creditors will use in the future to judge whether you are *credit-worthy* or not.

Should you be so careless as to mess up your credit while you are young, it could hurt your future chances of purchasing a car, or a home, or getting any kind of bank loan. Another little known fact is that potential employers sometimes run a credit check as well. They too want to know if you are trustworthy. Your credit report gives them an indication.

If you are using credit cards, request to see your credit reports at least once a year. Check for errors and make sure every detail is correct. On your report will be your credit score. It's important for you to know what that number is. If you want to know how the numbers are applied, check the list below:

Good credit score: 680 to 719

Average credit score: 620 to 679

Poor credit score: 580 to 619

Bad credit score: 500 to 579

The absolute worst credit score: Less than 500

You will hear some adults advise you that you must get a credit card to establish your credit. However, it would be better to never have a credit card at all than to have one, misuse it, and damage your credit.

Be aware of the pitfalls and act accordingly.

What Is FICO?

Ever wonder why your credit score is known as the *FICO score*? Here's the answer.

In 1956 a pioneer credit score company was set up as Fair, Isaac and Company. It was created by two men – an engineer named Bill Fair, and a mathematician named Earl Isaac. The company's headquarters were in San Rafael, CA, U.S.

The two founders began selling their credit scoring system a short two years after the startup. Similar systems soon followed. The company was later renamed Fair Isaac Corporation. FICO (the acronym for Fair Isaac Company) became the more well-known name.

The first *general-purpose* FICO score was used in 1989 by Equifax. Soon it was being used by all reporting agencies. The company went public in 1987. The stock market ticker symbol is FICO.

Now you know! You can amaze your friends with your trivia knowledge about the FICO score system.

CHAPTER 9: NOTE TO PARENTS ON THE ALLOWANCE QUESTION

Different Viewpoints

Probably no two families will agree on the allowance question. The decision of whether or not to extend an allowance to a child will depend on many circumstances. Some families simply cannot afford to fork over money to the kids on a regular basis. Others are of the opinion that the kids should earn their own money doing work outside the home. Still others want the allowance system to be tied to the weekly job list— in essence the allowance is payment for jobs completed. Then there are those who don't want to be bothered with any kind of *system*. They're more comfortable in giving out money on an as-needed basis. Less hassle, in their opinion.

Another aspect of the allowance question is the agreement or disagreement between the parents themselves. The failure of having a *meeting of the minds* can upset everything. Some parents have bad memories of childhood money situations. When May was a child, she would save money from her allowance, and then her mother would *borrow* from May's savings and never pay the money back. As one could imagine, May's bad experience with getting an allowance now affects how she deals with her three children.

A Look at the Reasons

It's so easy to get bogged down in a million different opinions and points of view, but let's move away from the emotional aspects and get down to basics. What is the underlying reason to give a child a set sum of money on a regular basis? The reason should be to teach that child financial responsibility. It should be to allow the child to make his own decisions with a small amount in the beginning, and thereby sometimes make a mistake with a small amount.

Once jobs are connected to the allowance, now the underlying principle has moved from learning financial responsibility to learning about working for a set wage. They are two different ideologies. This is often where parents get their focus blurred.

"Well, I can't see just handing over money to my children for nothing in return," says one parent. To this parent it seems like a free-lunch setup.

Again, the focus has been blurred. The *something in return* is to bring up that child to become a financially responsible teenager and young adult. What a reward that will be for the entire family to enjoy. And the best time to formulate those good spending and saving habits is when they are still in primary school.

How to Separate

This is not to detract from the need to have the younger set be involved in daily chores. But the question is, should they expect to be paid for each and every chore? If that becomes a pattern in the home on a daily basis, things can get tedious. When it's time to put away the groceries, fold the laundry, and set the table they may be asking, "How much will I get paid?"

Then if that same parent hands over money anyway – even when that child sits around and refuses to work – what has been accomplished in the way of creating good habits?

In the Stratton household, parents Dave and Korene started the allowance system when their four children were young. "With four children in the home," says Dave, "we need everyone to pitch in and help." The children are expected to keep their rooms clean, sort their own laundry, help with meals (especially clean up), take out the trash and so on. A weekly job list keeps them straight on who does which chore when.

However, for larger jobs such as raking leaves, mowing the lawn, washing the car, and washing windows, Dave and Korene are willing to pay extra above their allowance. This enables them to save up for bigger ticket items.

This system works well for the Stratton family and they feel it helps keep the paid-for-work aspect separate from the money-education aspect.

When to Begin

How young is too young to receive an allowance? Most families seem to agree that first grade (in the USA, about 6-7 years old) is a good time to begin. The child is learning about the money denominations, and the values of each one. In the UK the fifty pence coin is larger than the £1 pound coin, and in the U.S. the five-cent nickel is a larger coin than the ten-cent dime. For a young child this can be confusing because they naturally think the larger coin should be worth more. This basic knowledge will be necessary as they start to make their own purchases.

Beginning at age six or seven works well because the child at that age has the capacity for reason. This is also a perfect opportunity to instil family values by explaining (for example) why a certain amount will go the church or a designated charity. Why a certain amount will be set aside in order to build up savings.

The best system for a child this young is to receive their allowance once a week. Some families even set a specific time – such as nine o'clock on Saturday morning. This helps to keep the system orderly and increases the child's anticipation.

Remain Consistent

Once the system is in motion, remain consistent. If for any reason you find you must skip a week, call a family meeting and explain (at their level of understanding) exactly why the allowances will not be forthcoming. If you skip a payment without letting them know why, you will be going back on your word and cause the child to lose trust.

Let Them Make Mistakes

At the beginning, almost as soon as the money is in their hands (or pockets) they will want to go shopping. This is understandable. You may have to grit your teeth as you watch them make poor buying decisions, i.e. the little toy is lost or broken two days later. While you can and should make suggestions, in the end it's best to let them make the mistakes. Later you can discuss whether or not that was a wise purchase decision. Let them tell you what they think now that the rush of excitement has waned.

This is yet another reason for them to set aside the amount designated for charity and for savings right away. Now it's not in danger of being spent on other things.

The best part of all of this is that as they mature they will become wiser in their spending habits. As you see this evolving, be sure to commend them. They need your encouragement.

How Much?

Another sticky question among parents is how much is the right amount for an allowance. Again, this depends on a number of variables. If you start out giving them more than your household budget can afford and later you have to back down, it can be a painful experience for all involved. It's better to begin where you know you can afford it, and then give periodic raises.

If a six-year-old begins with two or three pounds, give it to her in coins. Now she can learn to count the money, she can help put the coins in the selected places for charity and savings, and make her purchases with what remains.

What Does the Allowance Cover?

As the children move into their teenage years, the decision is not only how much the allowance should be, but what should the allowance cover? Some families feel their teen should, with her allowance money, purchase school lunches, snacks, smaller clothing items, toiletries, entertainment, and school supplies. With her savings, she can choose to spend on bigger items such as a smart phone, or concert tickets. How about petrol for the car?

Does your teen use the family car for her use? Or is it for family errands like taking her little brother to soccer practice? Who fills up the tank? Is there a set of rules to follow?

In this area no two families will be the same. If the reason for giving an allowance is to teach financial responsibility, this responsibility should grow each year. A good time to reassess might be at the beginning of each new school year. Go over the upcoming expenses and discuss what will be needed and how the responsibilities should be covered.

If the teen is expected to spend her own money for movie tickets, does that still hold true when the entire family goes to the movies for a family night out? The Chapman family created a compromise on this situation. Sam Chapman said that he and his wife decided that they would pay for the movie tickets for the family, "...but then our two teenagers were expected to pay for their own snacks at the movie out of their allowance. They agreed, and it has worked out perfectly."

Arrangements such as the Chapmans' setup not only teach their kids about responsibility, but also about a sense of fairness and cooperation. Because the truth is, you cannot teach financial responsibility without teaching other character-building traits in the process.

As you give your teens more buying responsibility, one danger is to slack off and begin purchasing for them the very items you indicated would be theirs to cover. The next danger is to cave in and bail out when they come up short. Let them wiggle their way out of a tight situation a few times. That is all part of their learning process.

When your daughter shows you that designer jacket that she has her heart set on, but it's too expensive for her, discuss how the two of you might make it happen together. How much is she willing to pay? And how long is she willing to wait? (Oftentimes, when a teenager has to wait to make a larger purchase, in the meantime they will change their mind completely. Another good lesson learned.)

Allowance in the Wage-Earning Years

Once your teen lands that first job, or begins to do odd jobs on a regular basis, should the allowance continue or not?

It's such a relief for families when the younger set begins to bring their own money into the household budget. But don't be too quick to cut off the allowance. You may want to keep it going until the other income is more secure. First-time jobs and odd jobs can be sporadic and sometimes they can end just as quickly as they started.

One idea might be to cut back slowly the amount of the allowance as they start to earn an income. It can mean phasing out as the income increases. As long as the lines of communication remain open, you can come to a fair and agreeable solution to almost any money dilemma that comes up.

Pay for Good Grades?

Using money as an incentive for good grades can be a touchy subject. Most parents believe that good grades are expected, and that's that. Also there's the fact that what is a good grade for one student may not be a good grade for another. The ability to learn and achieve in academics will vary from one student to the next.

While this may seem trivial, there is a difference between using money as a motivator and using money as a reward. If your son has been struggling in maths and is continually getting low grades, but in one school term he brings that grade up, a monetary reward for his efforts would not be out of line. On the other hand, promising a certain amount of money if a certain grade level is achieved can create undue pressure.

Looking at the reason behind the action is a great qualifier. Ask yourself if you are using money to coerce and manipulate. If so, you may want to work on your own money attitudes. Keep in mind your long-range goal is to teach your teenager a healthy attitude toward money and finances.

Withholding the Allowance

Should withholding your child's allowance be used as a disciplinary method? Another sticky question. If communication is open and clear, if the child fully understands why the allowance is being withheld, and if the punishment fits the bad behaviour, and if you feel your child's behaviour is changed by this method, then by all means use it.

Be sure it is clear how much is being withheld and for how long. Will they miss one week's payment? Two?

An alternative to withholding might be to exact a fine on what they already have. Say it's Wednesday and you gave out allowance payments on Saturday. The child openly disobeys. Instead of withholding the upcoming allowance which is still a few days out, exact a fine on the spot. Even if it's only a few pennies coming out of their reserve, it can still be painful.

One mum set up a system where each child was fined twenty-five pence every time they left a wet towel on the bathroom floor rather than hanging it up. She created a "Fine Chart" and tacked it up on the refrigerator where all could see. It doesn't take very many fines before bad habits are broken and new good habits are formed.

The more they understand the value of their money and know how much it takes to purchase what they both want and need, the more effective money discipline will be. The key is to always be up front, and be fair.

Bottom line, the use of an allowance is far and away one of the easiest and most successful ways in which to teach kids the many aspects of financial literacy. It can start at first grade and follow them all the way up until they graduate from secondary school. Even if your children are already in their middle school years, it's not too late to start to set up a workable system.

The point is, at least try it. You owe it to yourself, your family, and especially to the kids to at least give it a go. You'll never know how much it can teach them until you actually set it in motion.

Now you can hand the book back to your son or daughter. We are now moving into Part III – *How to Multiply Money.*

PART III: HOW TO MULTIPLY MONEY

MULTIPLY MONEY

One of the saddest indictments of this present culture is that today's teenagers know how to spend money (they may not spend it wisely, but they do spend it), but they are almost totally ignorant of how to make their money grow. They have little comprehension of how to make their money go to work for them.

In Part III of *Financial Literacy for Teens and Their Parents*, I hope to change that. Once young people catch the realization of how money grows, they get excited. They quickly catch the vision and are ready to run with it. (Much more so than with the adult generation.)

One of the best things you have going for you, because you are young, is time. The earlier you begin to set your money to work for you, the longer span of time you will have to see some major mind-boggling growth.

Before we continue on this section about seeing your money multiply, take a look at the following graphic example. A young university graduate by the name of Darinda was surprised upon graduation to receive a gift from her favourite uncle; a tax-free gift of $10,000 (about £6,250). She could have bought herself a car, or splurged at a few high-dollar fashion shops. But she didn't. Instead, she invested it in an index fund. (Details on index funds coming up in a later chapter.) To Darinda's way of thinking, the money was a surprise, she wasn't expecting it, so she chose to put it away, and put it to work. With the $10,000 earning 11% a year here's what happened:

Age 21 - $10,000

Age 30 - $25,600

Age 40 - $72,600

Age 50 - $206,200

Age 60 - $585,600

Age 70 - $1,662,700

Safe to say that Darinda, unlike many others in today's society, would not be worrying about money in her retirement years. This is the power of compound interest.

Speaking of interest, we'll begin this section on growing money by learning about interest. What is it and how does it work? Let's get going.

CHAPTER 10: INTEREST

The subject of interest has been mentioned a few times already in the course of this book. You now understand how interest is charged on a mortgage when the family purchases a home. (The same thing is true when you purchase any item and make instalment payments – such as your first car.) You also are now fully aware of the insidious way in which credit card companies charge unreasonable interest rates and how they are compounded not monthly, but on a daily basis. Now it's time to turn the tables. What if that interest were working *for* you instead of against you?

One of the first experiences you will have with interest will probably be with the savings account that you opened with your local bank. Most savings accounts pay interest on the deposits, which means that your money is making money. Granted this will be a small amount, but it will help you to see that interest does not have to work against you.

We'll create an example for sake of illustration. Let's say that your grandparents set up a savings account for you and they deposited £1,000 into the account. Now we'll say that this financial institution pays five per cent interest on such an account. (That's higher than you can currently expect, but again this is for illustration.)

At the end of your first year, your account will now contain £1,050. You have earned fifty dollars. That is fifty dollars that you did not have to work for; it came to you because you allowed the money to stay in a place where it is working *for you.*

In the following year, the interest will be computed not just on the original £1,000 but on the full amount of £1050. This means your account will earn £50 interest on the original deposit, but it will also earn £2.50 on the £50 interest. That's right, you are earning interest on your interest. If you will remember from our discussion of credit cards, this is known as compound interest.

This quote has been attributed to Albert Einstein (whether or not he said it does not detract from the truth):

"Compound interest is the most powerful force in the universe."

No matter who said it, it is indeed true that compound interest is powerful. When left to grow, it just keeps on growing. Let's continue with our illustration.

If you left your £1,000 in this same account and if the interest stayed the same, after five years you would have earned a total of £276.28. Again, this is almost three hundred dollars that you did not have to work for.

Think what would happen if, through your own savings, you continued to add to this original £1,000? If you only added a few dollars every week, not only will your account grow, but so will your interest earnings.

Certificates of Deposit (USA)

In the USA, a step up from a simple savings account is a certificate of deposit—also known as a CD. (Obviously this term was in use long before anyone had ever thought of compact discs which are also called CDs.) A bank CD is a certificate issued by a bank when you agree to deposit money for a specified length of time. In other words, this might work well for your university fund since you aren't planning to withdraw it or spend it anytime soon.

Bank CDs can be for six months, a year, three years or longer. The advantage of a CD is that the interest rates will be higher than with your savings account. Since you agree to keep your money in the bank for a longer period of time, this means they can use your money in their own investments. They then are willing to pay a higher rate of interest.

It's important to ask a lot of questions before choosing to go with a bank CD. For instance, if you were to set up a six month deposit agreement, would the bank charge you a penalty if you had to withdraw funds due to an emergency? You need to know this ahead of time.

Some depositors who have large sums to deposit choose to *ladder* their CDs. If they were investing $20,000 for instance, they may choose to put $5,000 in a six-month CD, another $5,000 in a one-year CD, and so on. This way when the six months is up, that CD which has now matured, can be rolled over into a new CD. Keep in mind the further out the CD maturity date, the higher the interest being paid.

In the UK you can get savings accounts that tie up your money for different lengths of time; with 90-day accounts (for example) giving more interest than "instant access" accounts... in exchange for your 90 days notice of any withdrawal.

Money Market Account (USA)

Another option that USA banks offer is what is known as a money market account. This account usually offers interest rates that are almost double what a CD or an ordinary savings account earns. The accounts are a combination of a savings account, a checking (current) account, and an investment opportunity.

The requirements stipulate that you maintain a minimum amount in the account (which could be anywhere from $1,000 to $10,000) and the bank sets strict limits on the number of cheques that can be written and the number of withdrawals per month. The more money you have in a money market account the higher the interest it will earn. This means as your account grows over the years, so will the interest rates.

Check with your bank to see exactly what is offered in this type of account. There is no harm in having part of your money in a current account or savings account, and another part in a money market account. Do a little calculating and see where you can earn the most return on your money.

Individual Savings Account (UK)

In the UK there are special kinds of savings accounts called Individual Savings Accounts (ISAs) that allow you to save in a tax-efficient manner; i.e. you do not pay the tax that you would normally pay on any interest that is credited to your account.

True ISAs require the account holder to be 16 or over (for a Cash ISA) or 18 or over (for a Stocks & Shares ISA); but there are also Junior ISA variants of both. As just hinted, ISAs can be used to *invest your cash* (like any other savings account) or to invest in *stocks and shares*.

Interest Working for You

These are yet more examples of how interest can work for you. One other note while we are on the subject of interest is: any interest that you *never have to pay*, is money back in your pocket. Let's say you are ready to buy your first car. Instead of looking for the lowest monthly payments (which is how most people shop for a car), plan ahead and save as much as you can toward your purchase. The bigger the down payment you can make, the smaller the balance. The smaller the balance, the less interest you will pay. The less interest you pay, the more money you have to invest and make work for you! This is what financial literacy is all about!

CHAPTER 11: BONDS

Municipal Bonds

When a community wants to grow, perhaps by building a new swimming pool, or a city park, or playgrounds, they need money to make those improvements. Where will they get the money? Taxes won't always cover such expenses since taxes are designated for other expenditures such as road repair.

The solution is to borrow money from people by issuing bonds, which in this case would be known as municipal bonds. When an individual purchases a bond, he (or she) is *loaning* money to the entity that issued the bond. When the bond is held for a certain number of years, interest is paid out on the bond. Owning bonds is a type of investment.

Here's an example. A £5,000 bond at 6% interest will earn £300 a year. If that bond were held for twenty years that would equal £6,000. This means that, at the end of the term, the bond holder will receive back the original £5,000 plus the additional £6,000.

Another option for the bond holder is to have the £300 paid to them each interest period. Some people who manage large sums of money and are wise investors actually live off of interest payments. (How would you like interest to work that well for you?)

The longer the bond term (some are as long as thirty years) the higher the interest rate. This type of investment has a low risk.

While such municipal bonds may not be so prevalent (if at all) in the UK compared with the USA, the idea of a bondholder loaning money to an organisation serves our purpose as an illustration.

Corporate Bonds

Another type of bond is known as a corporate bond. These are issued by businesses that are either starting up or which plan to expand. Bonds are then issued to raise the needed capital. Corporate bonds usually pay a higher interest rate than municipal bonds, but also bring with them a higher risk. The risk is higher because sometimes businesses fail, in which case the investor could face a loss. But for the most part, bonds are safer than buying stocks. (More about stocks in the next chapter.)

Government Bonds

The third type of bond is a government bond. Nearly all countries offer some type of government bonds which are considered to be low-risk investments. In the UK these government bonds are called GILTS, and in the USA one can purchase treasury notes, treasury bonds, and treasury bills. Each one differs in length of term and how the interest is paid out.

Bond Ratings

To find out a bond's risk level there are bond-rating services that go to great lengths to research companies and governments to determine how safe the investment might be. For instance an AAA rating would be safer than a BBB rating and so on.

Bonds that are known as *junk bonds* are rated BB and lower. These may be issued by companies that are having a great deal of money problems. Perhaps these companies are going through a corporate structure change and may be able to succeed and grow. Or they may crash. People who invest in these types of bonds are willing to take the risk because of the possibility of earning more money on higher interest rates.

Purchasing a short-term, low-risk bond might be just the place for you to place your money while you are saving for university or for that first car. It will earn more than a savings account.

Bonds are just one more way in which your money can work for you, but you will need a financially literate adult to guide you as you take this step.

Now that you have a basic knowledge of bonds, in the next chapter you will learn more about stocks. Now it gets more exciting!

CHAPTER 12: STOCKS AND THE STOCK MARKET

Terms such as *stock, the stock market,* and *Wall Street* are heard every day. In nearly every newscast you will hear a report announcing that the stock market is up or down on that particular day. If you are a teenager whose family is acquainted with buying and selling stocks, you may already be familiar with this scene and have an understanding of what goes on. If that is true, you are definitely in the *minority.*

In spite of the fact that the stock market affects a wide range of financial areas on a global scale, most teens have little or no grasp on what it's all about. As a result, they lack the tools to move about comfortably in this arena. In spite of the enigma, it's not all that complicated. You may be in for a surprise if you thought otherwise.

Not only does the stock market affect the global scene, it can also be one of the avenues for learning how to put your money to work for you. Because of the immense importance of the stock market, this chapter is designed to help you to understand the basics.

If you were to purchase a *share* of a stock that you selected (we'll use Apple as a great example), you then become a *shareholder*, and you are now part owner in this gigantic corporation. Because your money is invested in the corporation, you are helping Apple to continue in business, to expand, and to research for future products.

The East India Company

The idea of multiple owners of a business is nothing new. In fact merchants were using this concept back in the 1500s. This was when fortunes were being lost because ships full of merchandise were lost at sea (which happened often when ships were much smaller and less seaworthy.)

A group of London merchants came together with the idea of forming a corporation which would limit the members' liability to whatever amount each had chosen to invest. If the ship went down, that amount would be all that could be exacted by the creditors. They named their corporation "Governor and Company of Merchants of London trading with the East Indies" (or simply, "The East India Company.") Perhaps you've read about the East India Company in your history books.

Due to the success of this endeavour more charters were granted by King James I and more trading companies were formed. Because risk was now reduced, more merchants were willing to launch out and business boomed in Britain. If the ship made it safely to its destination, sold the goods and made a profit, every person who invested received a fixed percentage of that profit. Their investments paid off.

Sometime later, when investing in a trading company, the individual would receive an actual stock certificate to show in detail what they had invested, on what date, and with which company.

Wall Street

So where is Wall Street in the U.S.? A newscaster might be heard to say, "The news today from Wall Street is…" Or, "Wall Street continued on its upward trend in trading today…" What are they talking about? Is there really a place called Wall Street where stocks are bought and sold?

In the colonial days of Manhattan, the Dutch built a wall in lower Manhattan to protect them from possible attacks from the British. A road ran alongside that wall. Later the wall was removed, but *Wall Street* remained. As the city of New York City began to emerge, a great deal of business was conducted in and around Wall Street. Although for many decades, Boston was the hub of the nation's financial district, in the early 1800s New York City (i.e. "Wall Street") took over that distinction.

An organized stock exchange was established in New York in 1792. The exchange was set up at 22 Wall Street, and was simply known as the Stock Exchange Office. In the early days trading wasn't open to the public as it is today. As a teenager, you would have been out of luck if you had wanted to invest in stocks in the 1700s. Only the elite adult men were allowed to participate. Out of these small beginnings, later would come the New York Stock Exchange.

Inevitably, those who were not considered the elite class, and who also wanted to have a part of the action, formed their own group. They were known as the Curbstone Brokers because they literally conducted their trading at the curbside. Rain or shine, they bought and sold to the common folk. While the *Big Board* – as the NYSE came to be known – set buying requirements at 100 shares, the Curbstone group allowed people to buy one share at a time. Again, catering to the common folk. Additionally, they brought in companies that were too small to be considered by their bigger brother, NYSE.

Because the action of the Curbstone trading was so fast, these traders formulated a type of *sign shorthand*. With hand signals, winks, nods, and head shakes, they *telegraphed* their intentions. Some of these hand signals remained in use on the trading floor of the Stock Exchange for many decades to come.

The Curbstone Brokers was the forerunner of the American Stock Exchange. Amazingly, they didn't move inside to a real office until 1919. At that time, they had spent almost 100 years outdoors. Such is the amazing history of the life of buying and selling stocks.

The UK equivalent of the New York Stock Exchange (NYSE) on Wall Street is the London Stock Exchange in the City of London.

What Affects Stock Prices?

Going back to what is heard on the news reports, the newscasters will say something like, "Apple was up three points today..." Or "Abercrombie & Fitch is down three points today..." What's going on here? What are these points, what makes them go up and down, and who cares?

Taking the last question first, those who care are the share holders. If you happened to hold hundreds of shares of Apple stock, you would be excited to know that your stock is now worth more today than it was yesterday.

In the world of stocks, one point refers to one dollar (or a unit of some other currency such as one pound or one pence in the UK). Sticking with dollars as the units used to price Apple shares; if Apple has gone up three points then the price has gone up three dollars. Simple. However, a loss or gain becomes more significant depending on the actual price of the stock.

We'll use a fictitious company called *Sports Shoes Unlimited*. SSU is selling for 20p-per-share. If the price goes up 3 pence it is now worth 23p-per-share.

Compare this to a stock that is worth 80p-per-share. We'll call this company *Greatest Smart Phone Corporation*. If GSPC shares go up 3p-per-share, you can quickly see that the percentage of growth for GSPC is much less than it is for SSU. The shareholder of SSU enjoyed a 15% increase, while the shareholder of GSPC saw an increase of 3.75%. Be careful not to confuse points with percentages of increase or decrease.

The remaining part of the question is what affects the stock prices? The answer is *almost everything*. Stock market prices can fluctuate due to bad news or good news; or because of a rumoured company buyout; or because of a nation's election cycle; or because of the announcement of a company's most recent earnings report. And the list goes on.

Human emotions also play a big part in stock market changes, especially the two biggies: greed and fear. When the majority of traders see a stock going up fast, greed kicks in and they want to jump on board and cash in on the action.

On the opposite side of the coin, when that same stock comes tumbling down, fear causes people to jump ship even if it means taking a loss. The wise traders who have been doing this for a lifetime understand how to ride out these gyrations and make money no matter if prices are going up or down.

But it's not the goal here to drill down into a study of stock analysis; the goal is to help you as the reader to have a basic knowledge of how the stock market works so you can consider one day becoming an investor yourself. At this point, it's sufficient that you understand points and percentages.

How Stocks Grow

As a company enjoys healthy growth, the public begins to have trust in that company. This would be a company that operates with integrity and makes wise business decisions within the company. (More about how to learn these details later.)

You would probably agree that Coca-Cola is one such company. Coca-Cola is known around the world; its logo is recognized by millions. If your father had purchased a share of Coca-Cola around 30 years ago, say in 1980, he might have paid about $0.69 for that one share. A short five years later, that share would have grown to be worth $1.49; it more than doubled. By 1990, his share would have then been worth $5.55. (Are you getting the picture here?) At the time of writing, in 2013, a share of Coke's stock is priced at $40.26.

Let's further imagine that your smart father did not simply purchase one share for $0.69 – instead, he purchased one hundred shares. His purchase would have come to a whopping $69.00. Today his stocks would be worth over $4,000. Can you see how given time this investment would have paid off in a big way? This is a prime example of making money work for you rather than you working for your money.

Stock Split

If you begin to pay attention to the financial news, you may hear that a certain company is announcing a *stock split*. That split could be *two-for-one*, which means for every share you own, you will now have two. This sounds pretty exciting at first, but then you learn that such an event didn't increase the value of your holdings.

If you had purchased 100 shares at £2-per-share, after the stock split you would have 200 shares valued at £1-per-share. Either way, you still have £200 worth of stocks. It's like cutting your birthday cake into smaller pieces to feed more people at your party.

If you aren't gaining monetary value, then what might be the advantage of a stock split? There are people out there who study the market in anticipation of stock splits. They watch for them. After a stock splits, more shares can be purchased for less money than before the split. Because this encourages trading, the stocks could see an increase in share price soon after the split. Because you are a share holder this could be of great benefit to you.

Some corporations refuse to split—Google being one of them. By watching closely, you will soon learn which companies will or will not create splits.

Going Public

What does it mean to *go public* with regard to the stock market? Basically it means making the change from being a private company owned by a few people to a public company (traded on the stock exchange) owned by thousands of investors.

The process of taking a company public is extremely complicated. As you might imagine, it involves reams of forms and reports. It involves an investment banker who works with the company to walk them through the steps. The investment banker will purchase all of the original stock, then turn around and quickly sell the shares to the public. Watching for promising companies to go public is yet another way to get on the ground floor of investing.

Wise Investing

It's a sad state of affairs when adults believe that information about investing is too complicated for teens to understand. Especially since most teenagers today know every detail of a dozen or more computer games.

Learning the inside workings of any publicly held company is much easier today that it has ever been. In the past, in order to learn more about a company, you had to write to or call the company and ask for an investor's report to be mailed to you. Not so today. Now you can go to the website of any company, from the oldest to the newest start-up, and learn all about how they run their business. Because they are *publicly held* entities, all of their information must be *public*. It's all there at your fingertips. It's up to you to take advantage of that information.

Surviving Downturns

You may be thinking that investing in the stock markets is extremely risky. There's a chance you could be wiped out and lose everything. After all, you've heard such stories yourself. In fact you may know someone personally who lost in a big way in the most recent crash of 2008.

It's true that there have been big losses along the way in the long history of the stock market. This is why using wisdom and discretion – learning all you can about each stock you purchase – should be high on your priority list. Guard against greed and running after *tips* given by someone who *says* they have inside information. This is always a recipe for disaster.

This was especially true during what came to be known as the dot-com debacle. In a time when tech companies were new, imaginative, and alluring, many start-ups grew too fast to be stable. Anyone with an Internet business idea could find willing investors. Greed took over; the stock prices soared. Built on a shaky foundation, it was inevitable that it all would come crashing down. Before it was all over, people lost great sums of money.

The flip side of this crash is that during the *mania* time, a great deal of research and discovery took place. Much of what we enjoy in the Internet today is a direct result of those early risk-takers. Even in the face of great losses, there is always something to be learned.

Strong, Stable Companies Hold Steady

During the worst market downturns, the strong and stable well-known companies act like anchors for the stock market. Though they may experience rough waters, they come out on the other side shaken but unscathed.

This is why it's always good to diversify. (More about diversification in Part IV.) If you have a desire to throw caution to the wind and invest in a new company that is on the cutting edge with fresh new ideas, do so with only a small fraction of your investing bankroll. And never invest money that you cannot afford to lose. In other words don't invest money that needs to go toward rent, groceries, or the car payment.

While it's impossible to give a thorough tutorial on stock market investing in this book, it's my hope that this beginner information has lit a spark inside of you. Once your curiosity is aroused, you can do your own study and research.

Did you know there are online sites that offer simulated trading exercises? Before the days of the Internet this was called *paper trading* where you bought and sold stocks logging everything on paper forms. No money involved. On the Internet, the exercises are even more realistic, and many sites also include educational materials to expand your knowledge about the stock markets. Run a search for "stock market simulation programs," and be amazed at what is available.

In the next chapter we will cover yet another way to multiply your money and that is through leverage.

Wading Through the Financials

Choose two or three stocks to watch. A good place to begin is selecting companies you do business with on a regular basis. Where do you buy your clothes? What is your favourite restaurant? What is your favourite fast food spot? What is your favourite make of vehicle? Start with these and begin a steady habit of following their activities. The more you watch and study the more familiar you will be with a company's activities.

One site that you can use to follow your stock selections is http://www.marketwatch.com/

Remember, the more you know about a company, the wiser you will be in investing. Here are clues as to what information is given and what it all means.

52-Week High/Low

These numbers tell the highest and lowest prices in a given year. Investors like to compare the highs and lows of a previous year with the current price. The company whose highs and lows are close together mean the growth is steady. If the numbers are far apart, the fluctuations are wider and may mean a more risky investment choice.

Div

This is the abbreviation for dividend. This is the dollar or pence amount (depending on currency) of the company's annual profits per share. This is what the company pays shareholders—rather like the interest you receive on your savings. Not all companies pay dividends, preferring to put that money back into the growth of their company.

Yld %

This refers to the yield percentage. It tells the amount of the dividend as a percentage of the stock's price.

Divide the dividend by the current price of the stock. If your stock choice criterion is high income, look for high yield. Compare the stock you are studying with others. You'll quickly see which stocks are high yield.

P/E Ratio

The Price/Earnings ratio is determined by taking the last price of the day for a share of stock, and dividing by the company's profits or earnings per share (EPS) for the last year. This number helps to determine if a stock is overpriced or underpriced.

Sales 100s (or Volume)

This number tells how many shares of that stock were traded. This trading information will help you to see if this stock is active or inactive. Because you are studying your choices over several months, you can note sudden increases or decreases in trading. These changes could be due to either good news or bad news. Heavy trading may be due to a news report that mentioned the company in a favourable light, resulting in a jump in the share price.

High/Low/Last

These figures simply tell the open and closing prices of a stock. Ordinarily there will be no large change in one day.

Net Change

The net change is the difference between the current price of a stock and the closing price of the previous day.

When you first begin to read the stock market reports, it will be like a foreign language. Don't let that stop you or slow you down. Soon these terms will be as familiar to you as all the details of your favourite computer games.

What are Index Funds?

An index fund is one of the simpler ways to invest your money at a low risk level. You've heard of a stock index such as the S&P 500. This is a group of the largest 500 companies in the US. There are other indices such as the Wilshire 5000, and the Dow Jones Industrial Average. (Similar indices exist in the global market.)

Someone came up with the brilliant idea of creating mutual funds that are tied to these indices. This means the fund is not invested directly in the stock market, but rather is based on changes of the prices in the index. Because over the years, the stock market averages nearly always go up, this is one of the most streamlined, and problem-free, manners in which to invest.

Those who aren't sure which criteria to use, can select a *balanced* index fund that will mimic a combination of categories which will include stocks and bonds. The balanced funds can create a complete diversified portfolio in one investment.

This is a great way for you as a teenager to get your feet wet in the world of stock investing. Once this step is taken, then you can graduate up to learning more about individual stocks and earn even more. Start small and work your way up.

The key is to *start!*

CHAPTER 13: LEVERAGE

Leverage is one of the least understood and least appreciated aspects of multiplying your money. There are numerous ways in which leverage can be applied in your life. It simply means doing more with less.

My First Experience Learning about Leverage

I had not been in London for very long when I was introduced to a type of business known as *network marketing*. This was totally new to me. As I entered this arena, I began surrounding myself with a different set of people. They were success-minded, success-oriented people. These associations changed my life.

In network marketing the concept was to not only sell products (in this particular company, I was selling training courses), but to recruit others to come into the company under me and be on my team. I then made a percentage of the commissions created by those under me. The more people I had in my group, the larger my commissions were. This is how leverage works. I was leveraging the work of those who were on my team.

I was quite accustomed to making a profit off items that I sold, but I had never heard of being able to make profits from the efforts of others. I was fascinated.

Later I learned the quote made by the famous American Oilman, J. Paul Getty (1892 - 1976) which explained this phenomenon: *I'd rather have 1% of the effort of 100 people than 100% of my own effort.* I quickly learned how true that was in my own life.

The company I worked with went to great lengths to train their representatives. I attended meetings where I heard new truths. One of these was: "Anything you want to do, or have, or be, someone has already done it. You can find a book about it, or take a course, or attend a seminar about it. You can learn from others."
Another truth I learned was this: "Decide what it is that you want to do with your life, find the person who does that and does it the best, and do what they do." This made sense to me. I could see how this would work for me.

I was unaware of it at the time, but I was now leveraging my life with knowledge. The more you know, the more you can accomplish. I was on a mission to learn everything I could about financial success.

My Second Experience with Financial Leverage

When I came into the network marketing business, I created my own company and registered it with the government. I learned that if you applied for a job, the officials wanted to know every detail about you, but if you create your own business, all they needed was your company name and address. It was much simpler.

I heard about a company that was selling telecommunication services who needed workers. They were marketing to companies rather than individuals, promising to lower their phone bills by 10%. This was exciting because I knew how to do that. I knew how to sell. Their representatives were paid a percentage for every account they signed up.

I then learned that this company encouraged their reps to hire others to work for them. Now I was even more excited. I contacted a friend I knew from network marketing and told him about my idea, and asked him to be my partner.

Together we set up an office and began to run ads for sales representatives from a local job centre. By the way, I went to the library and researched how to get an office rent-free. I learned that sometimes empty buildings just need someone – anyone – to set up a business. Perhaps they are renovating and will let you come in before the renovations are completed.

Not having any capital, I had no idea how I would pay my sales reps. This was when I learned that if I paid them on commission, no money would be paid to them until they made the sales. I was amazed. This was almost too good to be true.

Because my partner was a Brit, I let him interview our new recruits and train them. (My English was still very sketchy.) Within a few days, we had thirty sales reps going out knocking on doors to sell the phone-bill-saving product. We paid our sales representatives 50%, which made them even more eager to work harder. Within a few months I was making more money than I had ever seen in my life. I could have bought a new car every month.

I was leveraging our money and efforts through this team of workers. To this day, I am amazed that these concepts are not taught to our kids.

Another Example of Financial Leverage – Passive Income

Let's look at yet another example so we can expand on this idea of leverage even further. Ramona loved gardening and landscaping. As a high school student, she did afterschool and weekend work helping do yard work for those in her neighbourhood. She was especially busy in the spring when she helped people get their flower and vegetable gardens ready for the coming season.

By the time she graduated, Ramona had her own business. She wanted to grow her income, but she was limited to how much she could physically do on her own. One option was to begin hiring a crew to work with her. She didn't mind hiring students to help part-time, but she didn't relish the idea of all the paperwork that went along with having full-time employees. So Ramona took a different tack.

Realizing how many people were asking her questions about certain gardening techniques, or about her landscaping ideas, she turned to the Internet. Setting up a blog and several social media sites, she used her expertise to supply information to interested followers. At the outset, it was for the locals who knew her, but on the Internet there are no borders.

Her next step was to create a set of how-to books. It wasn't difficult to do — she simply used all of the blogs she'd been writing and turned them into books.

Now, while Ramona was still doing what she loved most – working with families and helping them to beautify their homes – she was also leveraging her expertise and earning passive income online at the same time.

Can you see how this could benefit nearly anyone who has an area of knowledge that others might want to know about? This is yet another great example of how to multiply your money – through passive income.

This section on how to multiply money is one of the most important simply because it's the gateway to financial freedom. It's my passion to teach this concept to as many young people as possible.

While learning to make your money grow is crucial, it is even more crucial to learn how to *keep* it. What good is it to have all this knowledge, and to build up a strong financial foundation, only to lose it because of failing to learn how to protect what you have? We'll learn more about that in Part IV.

PART IV: HOW TO PROTECT YOUR MONEY

PROTECT YOUR MONEY

In a perfect world you will go into adulthood, learn about money, make a lot of money, and live happily ever after. The problem is we don't live in a perfect world. The sad truth is just as soon as you accumulate a sizeable amount of money, there are people who will want to take it away from you. While you don't want to live in fear all your life – you want to enjoy your money – still you must use wisdom and close the door on as many possible ways to lose money as you can. This section will give you some basic guidelines to go by.

Some of these concepts will not be applicable to you for a few years to come, but it is vital that you become aware of them now. To be forewarned is to be forearmed. You want to be armed with knowledge that can be implemented, so you will not be blindsided simply because you were unaware. The first protection element will be protection from excessive taxation.

CHAPTER 14: TAXES

Taxes Are Everywhere

Governments, both local and national, stand ready to tax the money that you earn in as many ways as possible. And while all citizens want to do their part to support their home country, it's important to be aware of tax laws and not to have to pay more than your fair share. One of the ways to protect your money is to learn about tax shelters and deductions. Why spend your hard-earned money on taxes when you don't have to?

No matter your age, you have already been paying taxes for most of your life. In most countries some type of sales tax or Values Added Tax (VAT) is included when you make certain purchases. When you get a job you pay even more taxes, because certain taxes will be taken from your pay-cheque. Businesses and corporations are taxed, and in the UK, when a person dies, there is an inheritance tax. So taxes are everywhere.

Avoid Unnecessary Taxes

How can you know the best way to avoid unnecessary tax payments? There are a couple of possibilities. The first is to have a trusted accountant who can advise you. Accountants nearly always know the ins and outs of the tax system and can give you advice that can save thousands of pounds over the years.

Another possibility will be your mentor. We talked about mentors in Chapter 2. This is a person who does what you want to do, and has become a success in that area. You have now come under that person's tutelage in order to learn and grow. Because your mentor has walked the path before you, and because he is successful in a particular field, you can be fairly certain he knows about such things as tax deferment and tax shelters.

This is the time to ask questions. Learn as much as you can now. When the time comes you will be equipped to make the wisest decisions with regard to protecting your money against unnecessary taxes.

CHAPTER 15: INSURANCE

Car Insurance

Your first experience with insurance will probably be when you own your own car. Because teens are considered high-risk drivers, car insurance for your age group can be fairly expensive. Depending on your arrangement with your parents, you may have to pay for your own insurance. If so, you are already aware of how much it takes out of your pocket. In most countries it is against the law to drive without insurance, and a record of your coverage will need to be in the vehicle at all times. So you have little choice in this purchase. This is considered an unavoidable expense.

Consider for a minute how expensive it would be *not* to have this coverage. A vehicle is an extremely expensive purchase. Should you not have coverage, it might be impossible for you to replace or repair the vehicle in case of an accident

Add to this the fact that if you are involved in an accident which happens to be your fault, and if you are sued by the other party, it could require tens of thousands of pounds to settle. Sufficient coverage will cover those costs.

Contents Insurance

When you are out on your own the next type of insurance you may encounter is contents insurance to insure the things you own. You will be living in a dormitory room at university, or you will have your own apartment. You may not think you have many possessions, especially as a teenager just out on your own. But if you lost everything in some type of disaster, say a fire, you would be hard put to replace everything. Yes, your budget is tight, but shop around and seek out the best rates for your situation and purchase at least the most basic contents insurance policy. If you deal with an agent for your car insurance, perhaps she can also add contents insurance in with those premiums. Check and see.

If you have any electronics at all, consider how much it would take to replace what you might lose in a disaster. Would you be able to afford to replace them? This is why insurance is yet another way to protect your money.

Critical Wealth Protection

As you move into new situations as a home owner, as a business owner, as the head of a household, well-thought-out plans for insurance will be critical.

Many families have been left destitute upon the death of the family breadwinner. The salary which that person brought into the household is gone, and now the remaining spouse must somehow work to replace it. A sufficient life insurance policy would go a long way towards getting such a family past this kind of catastrophe. A trusted insurance agent can create the coverage plan that will be best suited for your needs.

Frivolous Lawsuits

We live in a litigious culture where frivolous lawsuits can come against a business or an individual for seemingly no reason at all. If a suit is brought against you, and even if you eventually win the case, you may be out thousands of dollars in court costs and attorney fees. This is not how you want to spend your hard-earned money. Here again, there are insurance policies that you can put in place to put up a wall of protection.

Some business owners set up trusts then place their business under the umbrellas of the trust structure. This also works to protect assets and wealth from unscrupulous lawyers.

Again, the point is not to keep your head in the sand and believe such things can never happen to you. That's what everyone says who finds themselves in such a predicament. Better to be aware, and prepared, way ahead of time. You'll sleep better at night.

CHAPTER 16:

DIVERSIFICATION

Diversify Your Holdings

"Don't put all your eggs in one basket." This little idiom is known in nearly every culture and nearly every country. It can be applied to many situations, but for this discussion we want to apply it to how you invest your money. One way of protecting what you have is to diversify your holdings. This means a percentage of your money might go into low-risk, high-liquidity investments. Another percentage might to into a higher-risk investment. You may want some in stocks, and have property investments as well.

When Greed Takes Over

When reading about people who suffer in an investment disaster, what usually has happened is this: An individual hears of an opportunity in which they can *make a killing* in a very short time. Because this opportunity is so great, and it's a *once in a lifetime* deal (or so the proponents are saying), the investor will take all he has and put into this one investment. If the opportunity goes sour, that person has lost everything. Not a wise move.

It would seem ludicrous that anyone would do such a thing. It sounds crazy. Why would someone risk everything? But they do. And they have... for centuries. It only takes a quick review back through history to find accounts of such events. As recently as the dot-com boom, that's exactly what happened. The tech stocks were going up so fast, and it looked like such a sure thing. People threw caution to the wind and put all the money they had into such stocks. When they came crashing down, the investors lost everything.

How much wiser it would have been to have invested a small percentage and then sold at a time when a nice profit could be taken out. But when greed comes in, wisdom goes out the window.

The best way to protect your wealth holdings is to keep them balanced by incorporating a variety of investment choices. If for some reason one should fail, you are still on a solid foundation.

CHAPTER 17: IDENTITY THEFT

Sophisticated Thieves

One of the plagues of this age of technology is that thieves are much more sophisticated. While it's impossible to be totally protected against such unscrupulous individuals, there are many preventative steps that can be taken.

You would probably never think of walking away from your car with the keys still in the ignition and the doors unlocked. You wouldn't leave the door of your house unlocked. Many homes have safety locks on the windows as well. Some have alarm systems. These are all precautionary measures to maintain safety. Now translate that behaviour over to your identity.

What the Thief Looks For

First of all, what is the identity thief looking for? It's your everyday transactions such as bank and credit card account numbers, your Social Security (or other identification) number, your name, address and phone number. Any other sensitive information they can find to use without your knowledge. When this happens it can take years to clean up the mess such thieves can make.

Monitor your Accounts

How can you tell if you've become a victim? One way is to constantly stay on top of your financial records. Monitor the balances of your accounts. Be on the lookout for unexplained charges or withdrawals. Other indications might be the denial of credit for no apparent reason. Or if you receive calls from debt collectors about items you never purchased. In other words, keep abreast of all your records and in that way any irregularities will immediately come to your attention.

Use Caution with Private Information

Always manage your personal information with caution. It's especially tempting to give out your information online. Identity thieves are especially good liars. You may think you are in contact with a bank representative, or a legitimate representative of a legitimate organization, when that's not who it is at all. Never be too quick to give out your personal information.

If your credit card is lost or stolen, immediately call the company and report the incident. Don't wait. As soon as they are made aware they will not accept any charges made on that card.

Other precautionary measures might include:

- Shred bank or credit card statements or any private records before putting them in the trash.

- Give out your private information only when necessary.

- Pick up your mail promptly from your mailbox (if outdoors). Never leave it to pile up.

- Never give out private information over the phone, through the mail or on the Internet unless you're absolutely confident of whom it is you're dealing with.

- Never share PIN numbers or passwords, even with people you believe you can trust.

- Ask for periodic checks of your credit reports to make sure all the information there is accurate.

The main point here is to use common sense when dealing with your own personal information. The thieves are out there looking; you can take extra steps to make it extremely difficult for them. Don't be an easy target.

Learning how to respect money and how to earn money is important, but it's all for nought if you don't put safeguards in place to protect your money. Respect it enough to protect it. You'll never regret the extra effort it takes to do so.

CONCLUSION

We have come to the end of our journey together as we have covered some of the most basic aspects of financial literacy for teenagers. Thank you for coming along.

It is my hope that along the way you have read about something that sparked your interest and made you want to learn more. And then learn even more. The most successful people in any field of endeavour are what are called *life-long learners.* They never stop learning. And you should never stop learning about finances. The more you know, the more you will always be in control of your own personal finances

Learn to respect money. Learn your own spending habits and take the necessary steps to exchange careless and mindless spending to wise and calculated spending. Continue to learn how to make your money grow. You always want your money working for you, instead of you working for money.

Never believe the myth that more money will solve all your problems. While it's nice to have money – better than being broke – if you have never learned how to manage money, it won't matter how much you have.

Sooner or later your poor spending habits will take over and you stand to lose it all.

I want to hear from you and know what is working – or what's not working – in your financial world.

You can contact me here: www.financialliteracyforteens.com or email at: info@financialliteracyforteens.com.

PART V: ACTION WEALTH SYSTEM

ACTION WEALTH SYSTEM

Could you become the next investment millionaire within the next five years and never have to work again?

Would you like the security of a regular income from just a few hours' work a week?

Would you like to learn simple but proven strategies that anyone can use—even starting with just couple of hundred pounds?

Do you want to clear your debts once and for all and have a realistic money-making system to help you achieve your financial goals?

Would you like to create money trees that would give you income whether you're awake or asleep?

How the Action Wealth System Works

It has been my pleasure taking you through the ins and outs of financial literacy for teens. I hope I have helped show you (and your children) the way to financial stability and success.

Some people believe that money is not the most important thing in life and, in fact, is the root of all evil. But some things are absolutely certain – money drives the world's economies, provides the foundation for our health services and is the cornerstone of equal education opportunities. In a nutshell, it improves our quality of life. So money IS crucial. If you have money, you have the option of either buying your slavery or your freedom. If you choose wisely, money can help you earn the freedom to live the life that you truly desire.

By understanding this early in life I became involved in business and from the age of nine spent many years trying to buy my freedom by sorting out the strong opportunities from the weak in the real world. It has been extremely providential and, in some instances, an act of fate how my entrepreneurial journey has enabled me to work alongside some of the best business minds in the world. My journey has propelled me to develop what is today my core business system—a system that I have used and continue to use to build and run several businesses (including my consulting business).

This system contains all the information and knowledge on various aspects of personal development, business development, entrepreneurial success, turn-key business systems, creating multiple streams of income, leadership and management, financial and asset protection, information systems, and personal and corporate responsibility. It also contains tried-and-tested tools that numerous individuals and businesses from all walks of life and across different continents have adopted as part of their income-generating structures. It is a system that can guide you towards becoming seriously good at what you do and, in turn, highly successful and able to compete.

I call this the Action Wealth System (TM). Why? Because without action, it may not be possible to achieve a wealthy or "healthy" personal or business system. The Action Wealth System is founded on the basic tenets of three programs. Depending on a few variables, the Action Wealth System can benefit you at the level that you are in as an individual or as a business.

The three programs are:

1. Self-Mastery Program
(Become the Best You Can Be)

Being able to stay motivated, develop a positive attitude and stay focused no matter what obstacles you face are the cornerstones of succeeding in life. This program will help you as an individual, or assist your employees. As an individual, you will learn to be motivated enough to make the first step or take any action you wish to take in life. As a business, your employees will learn how to avoid letting their limiting beliefs kill their dreams and, as a result, your dreams for the business. By identifying their strengths and weaknesses, you will be motivating them to become better and therefore ensure that your business thrives.

"Nothing can stop the man with the right mental attitude from achieving his goal; nothing on Earth can help the man with the wrong mental attitude." – Thomas Jefferson

2. Business Mastery Program
(Create Multiple Streams of Income)

Wealth = small efforts producing big results.

Lack of wealth = big efforts producing small results.

Usually the quickest and smartest way to build up your wealth stores is to:

a) Create multiple streams of income.

b) Live within your means and.

c) Accumulate assets rather than liabilities.

By understanding the above, you and your business are bound to be around for another 10 or 20 years. How many times do you get paid for every hour that you work? With the Business Mastery Program, you will master at least five key areas where you can get started to create additional sources of residual income for yourself. These areas will range from creation of information products; understanding the use of software systems/technology; investing in real estate; investing in stocks and shares; learning to market yourself; and starting your own successful turn-key businesses.

We focus on these main areas because we have studied them and understand how they work and how you can harness them in your favour.

3. Financial Mastery Program
(Protect Your Assets)

It happens every day; people make money and then lose it all, either by making poor investment choices, or spending it all on the wrong things. The Financial Mastery Program encourages long-term success. Regardless of how much income you have, if you can't live within your means, you will struggle financially.

One key reason why people remain poor is that they accumulate liabilities instead of assets. If you want to be rich then spend your lifetime accumulating assets – that is, things that put money in your pocket. This program is the final piece of the jigsaw for you and your business. With it you will learn about money and its worth, and how to protect the most important aspects of your life. You will learn all there is to know about asset protection – a method that many individuals and businesses use to protect their wealth. Plus, you will also learn how to use insurance and limited liability strategies to protect what you own. The basis of this program is primarily to emphasise the importance of keeping more of what your make in your lifetime.

Your NETWORK is equivalent to your NET WORTH.

As you can see, there is no such thing as a self-made millionaire. Part of living a wealthy lifestyle is knowing that you cannot do it by yourself; you must have a dream team behind you. That's what the Action Wealth System is all about. It is a dream team system designed specifically for you and your business.

For More Information please visit **www.actionwealthsystem.com**

Action Wealth System's Tools for Success

Super consultants strive for constant and never-ending improvement, so they keep investing in themselves. Take advantage of our success tools today to keep you on the road to success.

- Books

- Audio Books

- E-Coaching Programs

- Seminars and Workshops

- Personal Coaching

- Business Consulting

- On-Site Visits and Training

- Corporate Events and Conventions

- Geoffrey's Speaking Schedules

To order any of these products, visit our website at **www.actionwealthsystem.com**

Thank you.

ABOUT THE AUTHOR

GEOFFREY SEMAGANDA runs a global business training and consultancy firm that helps companies around the world run more efficiently, productively and profitably.

A respected entrepreneur, speaker, author and philanthropist, he is the founder and CEO of the Action Wealth Group of companies (Action Wealth Academy, Action Wealth Conference, Action Wealth Systems, Action Wealth Real Estate Development) and also a spokesperson for his own non-profit initiatives focusing on Youth Business Development, Clean Water Program and Give Blood. He has appeared on numerous TV and radio shows all around the world and has educated more than 500,000 people through his personal and business development courses and live seminars.

Geoffrey started making a profit at the age of nine to support his family during the war in his home country of Uganda. He moved to Europe in his early teens and established his first business at the age of 16; and by the age of 21 he had established five successful businesses in three countries. Today he often shares the stage with some of the best personal and business development speakers in the world. His other books include

The Action Wealth Creation System: *How to Be the Best, Create Multiple Streams of Income, & Make your Month Work for* You

*It's **Time** for Your Message: How to Position, Package and Promote Yourself as an Expert*

Lead in Your Chosen Field as a Super Successful Business Consultant

ALSO BY GEOFFREY:

How to Start Your Business the Right Way
50 Profitable Businesses to Run from Home

You can contact Geoffrey here:
Web: **www.financialliteracyforteens.com**
Email: **info@ financialliteracyforteens.com**

Meet Geoffrey, and receive free personal and business development at **www.actionwealthacademy.com**

FINANCIAL LITERACY GLOSSARY

A

Amortization: The process by which loan payments are applied to the principal, or amount borrowed, as well as the interest on a loan according to a set schedule.

Annual Percentage Rate (APR) : The finance charge or total amount it costs per year to use credit, calculated as a percentage of the amount borrowed (percentage rate), including interest, transaction fees, and service charges.

Annual Percentage Yield (APY) : The actual interest rate an account pays per year with compounding included; calculated the same way by all banks and other financial organisations.

Appreciation: A rise in value or price.

Assets: What a person owns, such as cash, stocks, bonds, property, and personal possessions. This is something that puts money into your pocket.

B

Back-end load: A sales charge paid when investments are sold.

Bait and switch: An illegal sales technique in which sellers advertise a product with the intention of persuading customers to buy a more expensive product.

Bankruptcy: Legal process for selling most of the debtor's property to help satisfy debts that can't be repaid, in exchange for (a) relieving debtors of the responsibility of paying their financial obligations or (b) protecting them while a plan is created and they try to repay debts.

Budget: A plan for managing money, dividing up expected income and expenses among spending and saving options based on personal goals during a given time period.

Business plan: A description of a company's organizational structure, staff, activities, marketing, and financial plans, including expected sources of income and expenses.

C

Capacity: The ability to repay a loan from present income; one of three factors in credit scoring.

Capital: The value of personal items that one owns, including savings, investments, and property, one of three factors used in credit scoring.

Capital gain: Income that results when the selling price of an asset is greater than the original purchase price.

Capital loss: Monetary loss that occurs when the selling price of an asset is less than the original amount invested.

Career: A profession or field of employment for which one studies or trains, such as financial services or medicine.

Cash flow: A measure of the money a person receives and spends.

Character: Refers to trustworthiness; one of three factors in credit scoring (e.g., paying bills on time shows financial responsibility). Creditworthiness indicates a responsible attitude toward living up to agreements.

Charitable gift: Aid to those in need.

Cheque or Check (USA) : Is a written order directing a bank to pay a person or business a specific sum of money.

Closed-end credit: A specific-purpose loan requiring repayment with interest and any other finance charges by a specific date. Examples include most mortgages or car loans.

Collateral: Property that a borrower promises to give up to a lender in case of default.

Collection agency: A business that specializes in obtaining payments from debtors who have defaulted on their loans.

Comparison shopping: The process of seeking information about products and services to find the best quality or utility at the best price.

Compensation: Payment and benefits for work performed; also payment to injured or unemployed workers or their dependents.

Compounding: Calculating interest on both principal and previously earned interest

Consumer: Buyers or users of goods and services for personal use.

Consumer economics: The study of the role of the consumer in an economic system.

Contract: Legally enforceable written or oral agreement between two or more parties to do or not do something.

Credit: Amount of money a creditor is willing to loan another to purchase goods and services, based on trust and the expectation that the money will be repaid as promised with interest.

Credit card: Card that enables holder to charge expenses for purchases or to get money, often with interest; synonymous with "buy now, pay later."

Creditworthiness: A measure of one's ability and willingness to repay a loan.

Credit rating/score: A measure of creditworthiness based on an analysis of the consumer's financial history, often computed as a numerical score, using the FICO or other scoring systems to analyze the consumer's credit. A creditor's evaluation of a person's willingness and ability to pay debts as judged by character, capacity, and capital; a mathematical model used by lenders to predict the likelihood that bills will be paid as promised.

Credit counselling service: An organization that provides debt and money management advice and assistance to people with debt problems.

Credit report: An official record of a borrower's credit history, including such information as the amount and type of credit used, outstanding balances, and any delinquencies, bankruptcies, or tax liens.

Credit score: A statistical measure of a loan applicant's creditworthiness, which is the likelihood of repayment.

Credit union: A not-for-profit financial cooperative that provides financial services to its member-owners, who have met specific employment, residence, or other eligibility requirements.

Creditworthy: The presumption that a specific borrower has sufficient assets, income, and/or inclination to repay a loan.

D

Deductible: The pound amount or percentage of a loss that is not insured, as specified in an insurance policy.

Default: The failure to meet a financial obligation or agreement.

Dependent: A person who relies on another individual for support.

Disposable income: Gross pay minus deductions for taxes.

Dividends: Earnings from corporate stock or credit union share accounts.

Debit card: Card used to pay for goods and services directly from a current account (UK) or checking account (USA) by transferring funds electronically from one's bank account to the store's account to pay for a purchase.

Debt: Entire amount of money owed to lenders.

Depreciation: Decline in a product's value that starts the moment a product is purchased (e.g. a car).

Diversification: Distributing funds among different types of investments to minimize overall risk.

E

Earned income: Earnings from employment, including commissions and tips.

Easy-access credit: Short-term loans granted regardless of credit history, often for very short periods and at high interest rates.

Electronic Funds Transfer (EFT): The shifting of money from one financial institution account to another without the physical movement of cash.

Emergency fund: Money set aside for unexpected expenses or for living costs in case of job loss.

Employer-sponsored retirement savings plan: Tax-deferred investment programs, such as 401(k) plans for corporate employees and Section 457 plans for state and local government employees (in the USA), which provide, in some cases, employer matching funds. Typically "pension plans" in the UK.

Estate: The assets and debts that a person leaves at death.

Ethics: A set of moral principles or beliefs that govern an individual's actions.

Expense: The cost of goods and services, including those that are fixed (such as rent and car loan payments) and those that are variable (such as food, clothing, and entertainment).

Economy—global or world: Worldwide system that results from choices of consumers, workers, business owners, manufacturers, and government officials in multiple societies and with increasing trade and cultural exchange.

Employee benefits: Additional benefits, beyond a pay-cheque, offered by employers (e.g., health insurance or pension plan).

Entrepreneur: A person who owns and operates her or his own business. A person who creates a business from scratch, based on a need or personal expertise, and puts creativity and ingenuity into action to provide a service or product. A person who organizes, manages, and takes the risks involved in creating a new product/service or developing a better way to operate a business.

F

Fair Credit and Charge Card Disclosure Act: A part of the Truth in Lending Act (USA, but there is equivalent legislation in the UK) that mandates a description of key features and costs— such as APR, grace period, balance calculation, annual fees, and penalty fees—on credit card applications.

Fair Credit Billing Act: A federal law (USA) that addresses billing problems with open-end credit accounts by requiring, for example, that consumers send a written error notice within 60 days of receiving the first bill containing the error, and preventing creditors from damaging a consumer's credit rating during a pending dispute.

Fair Credit Reporting Act: A federal law (USA) that covers the reporting of debt repayment information, requiring, for example, the removal of certain information after seven or ten years, and giving consumers the right to know what is in their credit reports, to dispute inaccurate information, and to add a brief statement explaining accurate negative information.

Fair Debt Collection Practices Act: A federal law (USA) that prohibits debt collectors from engaging in unfair, deceptive, or abusive practices, such as calling consumers at work after being told not to.

FICA: Federal Insurance Contributions Act.

Finance charge: The total dollar or pound amount paid for credit. Example: A £100 loan repaid with £9 interest plus a £1 service fee has a finance charge of £10.

Financial adviser: A person who provides financial information and advice. Examples include employee benefits staff, bank and credit union employees, credit counsellors, brokers, financial planners, accountants, insurance agents, and attorneys.

Financial goals: Desired results from one's efforts to achieve personal economic satisfaction.

Financial literacy: The ability to use knowledge and skills to manage one's financial resources effectively for lifetime financial security.

Financial plan: A report that identifies a person's financial goals, needs, and expected future earning, saving, investing, insurance, and debt management activities; it typically includes a statement of net worth.

Financial plan, financial planning: Personal financial planning is the process of (a) setting goals, (b) developing a plan to achieve them, and (c) putting the plan into action. Ongoing thinking process to develop an orderly program or blueprint for handling all aspects of one's money, including spending, credit, saving, and investing.

Fraud: Intentional misrepresentation of information with the intent to deceive or mislead.

Front-end load: A sales charge paid when investments are purchased and sometimes when dividends are reinvested.

G

Garnishment: A court-sanctioned procedure that sets aside a portion of an employee's wages to pay a financial obligation.

Grace period: A time during which a borrower can pay the full balance of credit due and not incur finance charges or pay an insurance premium without penalty.

Gross pay: Wages or salary before deductions for taxes and other purposes

Goal: Statement about what a person wants to be, to do, or to have accomplished by taking certain steps; provides direction to a plan of action.

Goal setting: The process used to determine what an individual wants to be, do, or have, i.e., what a person wants to accomplish.

Green products: Products considered environmentally safe according to objective, authoritative testing.

I

Identity theft: The crime of using another person's name, credit or debit card number, Social Security number, or another piece of personal information to commit fraud.

Income: Money earned from investments and employment.

Individual Retirement Account (IRA): An USA investment with specific tax advantages. A traditional IRA defers taxes on earnings until withdrawal and, under certain circumstances, allows the deduction of some contributions from current taxable income. A Roth IRA requires after-tax contributions only, but allows tax-free withdrawals under certain rules.

Inflation: An overall rise in the price of goods and services; the opposite of the less common deflation.

Insurance:

Car Insurance – Provides liability and property damage coverage under specific circumstances.

Disability Insurance – Replaces a portion of income lost when a person cannot work because of illness or injury.

Health Insurance – Covers specific medical costs associated with illness, injury, and disability.

Homeowners Insurance – Provides property damage and liability coverage under specific circumstances.

Liability Insurance– Protects the insured party from others' claims of loss due to the insured's alleged or actual negligence or improper actions.

Life Insurance – Protects dependents from loss of income, debt-repayment, and other expenses after the death of the insured party.

Long-term care Insurance – Covers specific costs of custodial care in a nursing facility or at home.

Contents Insurance – Protects from losses due to damage to the contents of a dwelling rather than the dwelling itself.

Insurance premium: The payment a person makes to an insurance company in exchange for its promise of protection and help.

Interest: 1. Cost of borrowing money. 2. Earnings from lending money.

Interest income: Money that financial institutions, governments, or corporations pay for the use of investors' money.

Investing: Purchasing securities such as stocks, bonds, and mutual funds with the goal of increasing wealth over time, but with the risk of loss.

Investment: Setting aside money for future income, benefit, or profit to meet long-term goals; using savings to earn a financial return.

L

Lease: A written contract specifying the terms for the use of an asset and the legal responsibilities of both parties to the agreement, such as a landlord and tenant.

Liabilities: Amount a person owes, such as unpaid bills, credit card charges, personal loans, and taxes.

Living will: A document that contains the signer's desires for specific medical treatment in case the person is unable to make medical decisions; also known as a health care directive.

Loan sharks: Unlicensed lenders who charge illegally high interest rates.

Loss leader: Sales tactic where an item is priced at below cost price to attract buyers who will then purchase other merchandise.

M

Medicaid: A USA program, financed by state and federal government tax revenues, to pay specified health care costs care for those who cannot afford them.

In the UK, people may pay for private medical insurance or may rely on the state-funded National Health Service (NHS).

Medicare: A USA federal government program, financed by deductions from wages, that pays for certain health care expenses for older citizens. The Social Security Administration manages the program. In the UK, people may pay for private medical insurance or may rely on the state-funded National Health Service (NHS).

Money: Anything that is generally accepted as payment for goods and services; a medium of exchange; legal tender.

Mortgage: Loan to buy property such as land or a home.

Mutual fund: An investment tool that pools the money of many shareholders and invests it in a diversified portfolio of securities such as stocks, bonds, and money market assets.

N

Needs: Essentials or basics necessary for maintaining physical life, including food, clothing, water, and shelter, sometimes called material well-being.

Net worth: The difference between a person's assets and liabilities.

O

Open-end credit: An agreement with a financial institution that gives a borrower the use of money up to a specified limit for an indefinite time as long as repayment of the outstanding balance and finance charge proceeds on schedule; also known as revolving credit or a revolving line of credit. A credit card is an example.

P

Pawnshop: An easy-access credit business that makes high-interest loans secured by personal property collateral such as jewellery.

Payday loan: An easy-access credit business that makes high interest loans for the period of the borrower's pay cycle. This practice is illegal in some states.

Payment method: The means of settling a financial obligation, such as by cash, cheque, credit card, debit card, smart card, or stored value card.

Payroll deductions: Amounts subtracted from gross income that are withheld by an employer for items such as taxes and employee benefits.

Peer pressure: The influence that a social group has on an individual, based on the individual's desire for the group's approval.

Pension Protection Act: A (USA) federal law that attempts to strengthen employees' retirement security by, among other things, allowing employers to automatically enrol employees in retirement savings plans.

Personal finance: The principles and methods that individuals use to acquire and manage income and assets.

Philanthropy: The act of voluntarily contributing to others' welfare.

Point of sale (POS): The location where a transaction occurs. POS software can track sales, inventory, and customer information.

Portfolio: A collection of securities – such as stocks, bonds, mutual funds, and real estate – that an individual investor owns.

Principal: 1. An amount of money originally invested, excluding any interest or dividends. 2. An amount borrowed, or an outstanding loan balance.

Privacy: Freedom from unauthorized release of personal information.

Probate court: The government institution with jurisdiction over a deceased person's will and estate.

Prospectus: A legal document that provides detailed information about mutual funds, stocks, bonds, and other investments offered for sale, as required by the Securities and Exchange Commission.

Points—mortgage: A one-time service charge by mortgage lenders at closing to increase the return on the loan; each point is one percent of the amount of the principal.

Profit: The difference between the cost required to create a product or supply a service and the money received from selling it.

Purchasing power: The value of money measured in the amount of goods and services that can be bought with it.

R

Recordkeeping: The process of keeping an orderly account of a person's financial affairs, including income earned, taxes paid, household expenditures, loans, insurance policies, and legal documents.

Rent: A periodic fee for the use of property.

Rent-to-own: A plan to buy a product with little or no down payment by renting it until the final payment is made, at which point the total paid far exceeds the product's purchase price.

Repossession: Confiscation of collateral, often without notice, if a borrower defaults on a loan.

Risk management: The process of calculating risk and devising methods to minimize or manage loss, for example, by buying insurance or diversifying investments.

Rule of 72: A rough calculation of the time or interest rate needed to double the value of an investment. Example: To figure how many years it will take to double a lump sum invested at an annual rate of 8%, divide 72 by 8, for a result of 9 years.)

Resources: Human resources are those resources people have within themselves, such as working knowledge, skill, mental effort, motivation, energy. Non-human or external resources include money, time, and equipment.

Rate of return: How fast money in savings account or investment grows.

Risk—investment, personal, insurance: The probability of making a profit or losing money on one's investment; the chance an investment will decrease in value; possible losses involving income or standard of living. The possibility of a loss from perils to people or property covered by insurance.

Risk management: Deliberately and systematically using various strategies for controlling against potential personal or financial loss from pure risks.

Risk tolerance: The amount of uncertainty or possibility of loss the individual can bear.

S

Salary: Compensation for work, expressed as an annual sum and paid in prorated portions regularly— usually weekly, bi-weekly, or monthly.

Savings account: A financial institution deposit account that pays interest and allows withdrawals.

Savings bond: A document representing a loan of more than one year to the U.S. government, to be repaid, with interest on a specified date.

Security: 1. A legal agreement that records a debt or equity obligation from a corporation, government, or

other organization. Examples include stocks and bonds.
2. Collateral for a loan.

Simple interest: Interest calculated periodically on loan principal or investment principal only, not on previously earned interest.

Standard of living: The overall degree of comfort of an individual, household, or population, as measured by the amount of goods and services its members consume.

Stock: An investment that represents shares of ownership of the assets and earnings of a corporation.

Savings: Money set aside for short-term goals.

Scarcity: An economic condition created by an excess of human wants over the resources necessary to satisfy them; an inability to satisfy all of everyone's wants.

Shared risk—insurance principle: Using premiums from many policy-holders to reimburse the losses of a few, so that no one suffers a financially devastating loss.

Social security: The (USA) federal government's basic program for providing income when earnings are reduced or stopped because of retirement, or disability. Income is also provided to families when the working parent(s) dies and underage children are a part of the family. The UK National Insurance (NI) is equivalent.

T

Take-home pay: Gross wage or salary, plus bonuses, minus deductions such as for taxes, health care premiums, and retirement savings.

Tax: A government fee on business and individual income, activities, or products.

Tax credit: An amount that a taxpayer who meets certain criteria can subtract from tax owed. Examples include a credit for earned income below a certain limit and for qualified post-secondary school expenses.

Tax deduction: An expense that a taxpayer can subtract from taxable income. Examples include deductions for home mortgage interest and for charitable gifts.

Tax deferral: The feature of an investment in which taxes due on principal and/or earnings are postponed until funds are withdrawn, often at retirement.

Tax exemption: Earnings, such as interest from municipal bonds (USA) or Individual Savings Accounts (UK) that are free of certain taxes.

Tip: An amount paid for a service beyond what's required, usually to express satisfaction; also known as a gratuity.

Title loan: A high-cost, short-term loan that uses the borrower's automobile as collateral.

Transfer payment: Money that a government provides to citizens for reasons other than current employment or the delivery of goods or services in exchange. Examples include Social Security, veteran's benefits, and welfare.

Trust: A legal arrangement through which a trustor manages a trustee's assets for the good of one or more beneficiaries.

Truth in Lending Act: A (USA) federal law that requires financial institutions to disclose specific information about the terms and cost of credit, including the finance charge and the annual percentage rate (APR).

Truth in Savings Act: A (USA) federal law that requires financial institutions to disclose specific information about the terms and costs of interest-earning accounts—such as annual percentage yield (APY)—and certain other financial services.

Taxes: A compulsory payment by individuals/organizations to the government; fees placed on income, property, or goods to support government programs.

Time value of money: The relationship between time, money, and rate of return (interest), and their effect on earnings growth. The more time, money, and rate of interest, the more money yielded at the end of a period of time.

V

Values: An individual's beliefs about what is important, desirable, and worthwhile, which often influence decisions.

Value system: A set of criteria, standards, or principles that guide an individual or group's behaviour and which provide a sense of direction to life.

Vision—financial: Description of (a) how an individual defines future financial success and (b) what he/she wants to accomplish; provides direction for decisions and actions that invent the preferred future: What will the future look like if financial strategies are successfully implemented and one's full potential is achieved.

Volunteer service: Working to help others or one's community without being paid.

U

Unearned income: Earnings from sources other than employment, including investment returns and royalties.

W

Wage: Compensation for work, usually calculated on an hourly, daily, or piecework basis and paid on schedule—usually weekly, biweekly, or monthly.

Warranty: A written guarantee from the manufacturer or distributor that specifies the conditions under which the product can be returned, replaced, or repaired.

Wealth: Accumulated assets; positive net worth.

Welfare: Aid in the form of money or necessities for those in need; often from a government program.

Will: A legal declaration of a person's wishes for the disposition of his or her estate after death.

Wants: Items that a person would like to have but are not essential for life. Items, activities, or services that may increase the quality of life, but one can live without them.

Warranty: A company's promise that its product or service will meet specific standards over a given period of time, or the company will repair or replace it, redo the work, or give a refund.

Wealth-building: Increasing the total value of what one owns; one's tangible assets using strategies to increase savings and personal asset accumulation, thereby promoting individual/family economic well-being and financial security.

Withholding: Employer deductions from employees' earnings to pay employees' taxes.

Work, job: Employment, occupation, effort exerted to make or do something. On a relative basis, short-term work or tasks completed for pay.

ENDNOTES

[1] http://www.statisticbrain.com/teenage-consumer-spending-statistics/

[2] http://rbs-pocketmoney.co.uk/money/money-news/pocket-money-spending-habits.html

[3] http://www.guardian.co.uk/money/2010/mar/30/teenagers-expect-earnings-51000

[4] http://www.aboutschwab.com/images/press/teensmoneyfactsheet.pdf

[5] http://mufinancialtip.blogspot.com/2010/09/teens-and-money.html

[6] http://www.aboutschwab.com/images/press/teensmoneyfactsheet.pdf

www.ingramcontent.com/pod-product-compliance
Lightning Source LLC
Chambersburg PA
CBHW051451170526
45166CB00001B/204